WHAT IS YOUR I.Q. (Ice Quotient)?

Test it with these questions:

- Which high-scoring hockey player studied for the priesthood before turning to the ice lanes?

- Can you name Gerry Cheevers' other ambition in sports besides being the world's best goal-tender?

- What was the turning point of the 1973 Stanley Cup final between the Chicago Black Hawks and the Montreal Canadiens?

- How did The Stanley Cup become a part of hockey's lore?

You may not be in the "hockey genius" category yet, but you will be after reading the answers to these and other questions in

HOCKEY STARS OF 1974

STAN FISCHLER, author of a syndicated column, "Inside Hockey," also appears in *The Sporting News* where he writes "Speaking Out On Hockey." He has written numerous books including *Slapshot, Hockey's Greatest Teams,* and *Bobby Orr and the Big, Bad Bruins* among many others about hockey. He lives with his hockey-writing wife, Shirley; son, Benjamin; and pet puli, Chazy, in New York City. He is commissioner of the World Table Hockey Association and occasionally puts on the blades to refresh his feel of the ice.

HOCKEY STARS OF 1974

STAN FISCHLER

Research Assistants
MIKE RUBIN
STEVE MISHKIN

PYRAMID BOOKS • NEW YORK

To Benjamin, who goes both ways and is the real star of 1974

HOCKEY STARS OF 1974

A PYRAMID BOOK

First printing October 1973
Second printing January 1974

ISBN 0-515-03280-8

Pyramid Books are published by Pyramid Communications, Inc. Its trademarks, consisting of the word "Pyramid" and the portrayal of a pyramid, are registered in the United States Patent Office.

Pyramid Communications, Inc., 919 Third Avenue, New York, New York 10022

TABLE OF CONTENTS

THE SEASON PAST

THE 1972-73 period in professional sports was the year of the endless hockey season.

When the Boston Bruins won The Stanley Cup and the annual draft meetings were concluded in the Spring of 1972, instead of ending, the hockey season actually began again. And between June 1972 and October 1972 there appeared to be more hockey on the sports pages—not to mention the front pages—than during mid-Winter.

Two unusual factors caused this state of affairs. The first was the emergence of a baby major league, The World Hockey Association. The second was the truly fabulous eight-game series between the Soviet National Hockey Club and the National Hockey League-sponsored Team Canada.

Just days after the Bruins won The Stanley Cup in 1972, agents from the WHA began combing NHL rosters in their efforts to sign players for the new 12-team league. And with each week there seemed to be still another sensational story as NHL aces either threatened to, or actually did jump to the new league.

By far the most decisive development occurred in June 1972 when Chicago Black Hawks scoring leader Bobby Hull signed a ten-year $2,750,000 contract to play and coach the Winnipeg Jets. Hull's move made front pages across the continent and promptly forced the hitherto smug NHL owners to sit up and take notice, and to eventually take legal action.

Hull's switch inspired other NHL superstars to consider a change. A month later, Montreal Canadiens defenseman J.C. Tremblay signed with the Quebec Nordiques, while Boston Bruins goalie Gerry Cheevers left Beantown for the Cleveland Crusaders.

By now panic gripped the NHL front offices. Fearful of being raided, the New York Rangers signed all of their

7

better players to outlandishly high salaries, losing only defenseman Jim Dorey to the WHA's New England Whalers. The more frugal Bruins weren't as lucky. They lost Johnny McKenzie and Derek Sanderson to the Philadelphia Blazers and Teddy Green to the New England Whalers. The New York Islanders, who had yet to play a single NHL game, lost Norm Ferguson and Garry Peters to the New York Raiders and Ted Hampson to the Minnesota Fighting Saints, just to name a few. And so the raiding continued through the Summer.

Meanwhile, Team Canada went into training for the eight-game series—four in Canada and four in Russia—that supposedly would be a breeze for the NHL aces. "If we don't win this series in eight straight," said Montreal goalie Ken Dryden, "it will be a dark day for Canada, judging by the way people are talking."

It *was* a dark day for Canada. On September 2, 1972 the first game of the series was played at The Forum in Montreal and the Russians triumphed, 7-3. "This," said one NHL official, "is the catastrophe of the century."

The NHL skaters rebounded in the second game for a 4-1 win, but the third game ended in a 4-4 tie, and then the Russians humiliated Team Canada, 5-3, in the final game of the Canadian tour. Vancouver fans chased them off the ice with a resounding chorus of boos.

When the series resumed in Moscow, Team Canada opened with a 3-0 lead right up until the third period; but the astonishing Russians would not be denied and rallied for a 5-4 victory. "The Russians," said Dryden, "are not twenty guys dependent on a star to bail them out. They have an organized plan of attack that pays off."

Now it was Team Canada's time to rally. Trailing 3-1-1, the NHL skaters suddenly came alive and took the next three games and the series. Toronto Maple Leafs forward Paul Henderson emerged the hero, scoring the winning goals in the last minutes of the seventh and eighth games.

Despite the stirring comeback, Team Canada left Russia with the awesome realization that the Soviet skaters were every bit as good as the North American professionals, if not better. "The feeling," said Dryden, "seems to have changed to an awareness that the Russians have something going, too."

Once the Team Canada series had ended, attention turned to the war between the NHL and the WHA. Law suits brought by the NHL sidelined Bobby Hull through the early part of the season, but a Philadelphia judge finally ruled in favor of the WHA, and Hull joined the Winnipeg Jets as an active skater.

But Hull wasn't capable of filling all the WHA rinks all the time, and within a month of the opening game problems began surfacing in the new league. Despite the presence of Derek Sanderson, Johnny McKenzie, and Bernie Parent, the Philadelphia Blazers were a bust at the gate. Attendance also was a problem in New York and Ottawa.

"We expected problems," said WHA president Gary Davidson, "and have contingency plans to handle them."

By December, the WHA took over operation of the debt-ridden New York franchise. In Philadelphia, owner Bernie Brown of the Blazers made several economy moves, one of which involved eliminating Sanderson from the lineup. Eventually, he was granted a form of "severance pay" from the WHA and returned to the Boston Bruins.

There also were WHA bright spots. Quebec proved to be a solid franchise, along with New England, Houston, and Winnipeg. Houston and Los Angeles did better than expected while Cleveland, Edmonton, and Chicago kept their heads above water. Ottawa, which started with the worst gate in the league, rallied in the homestretch, but not enough to prevent a move to Toronto.

Despite raids and a lower quality of play throughout the league, the NHL enjoyed a financial bonanza in every one of its cities but Oakland, where Charles Finley's Seals cut ticket prices in half to woo customers. Atlanta, which iced a surprisingly strong squad, took to hockey like gin takes to tonic. Likewise, the New York Islanders attracted a large and devoted following of their own at Nassau Coliseum.

As for the races, the Rangers were favored in the East and the Black Hawks still rated high in the West, although Bobby Hull was gone. But Emile Francis' Broadway Blueshirts proved to be the most disappointing team in either division. They not only missed first place for the 31st consecutive season, they even relinquished second place to the Boston Bruins in the last weeks of the campaign.

Because they were in a year of rebuilding, the Montreal Canadiens were not expected to finish higher than second and certainly not expected to win The Stanley Cup. But coach Scotty Bowman had them cracking early in the schedule, and by early March it was clear that the Flying Frenchmen would win The Prince of Wales Trophy.

"It reached a point," said Canadiens captain Henri Richard, "where each of our losses was like a disaster. There will be even more pressure for us in the playoffs."

The Canadiens lost only ten out of 78 regular season games. In the West Division Chicago's Black Hawks won The Clarence Campbell Bowl with a less impressive record (42 wins, 27 losses, nine ties) but still cleared second place Philadelphia by eight points.

Considerably more balanced than the NHL, the WHA offered a stimulating race in its first season. Bobby Hull's Winnipeg Jets won in the West and Teddy Green's New England Whalers were the class of the East. Not surprisingly, the same teams met in the WHA playoff finals for the Avco Cup. Fortified with more seasoned former NHLers, New England won the championship four games to one.

The NHL's Stanley Cup playoffs offered the Rangers a chance for redemption for their disappointing play during the regular season. In the opening round the Broadway sextet responded with an easy five-game rout of the defending champion Bruins.

In other rounds, Chicago knocked out St. Louis, as expected, Buffalo gave Montreal a scare before bowing four games to two, and Philadelphia eliminated Minnesota. As the semi-finals got under way, the Rangers were favored over Chicago; and Montreal over Philadelphia.

Both the Flyers and the Rangers won their opening games on enemy ice but never won again. Chicago stunned the Rangers with four straight triumphs, while the Canadiens, more or less, did as expected against a hard-hitting Philadelphia club.

"We had to win," said Henri Richard. "After finishing first our fans expected us to win The Cup. By the time we reached the finals we had to win The Cup because, by then, they had forgotten that we finished in first place. When you are the Canadiens you cannot make excuses."

The Canadiens and Black Hawks had played a seven-game final in 1971 before Montreal annexed The Cup. This time it took six games for the Canadiens, who at times appeared shaky, but always the better team.

"We made a great effort," said winning coach Bowman. "We had a great team and it was a great series."

Whether Scotty was right or wrong didn't seem to matter. Everybody breathed easier at the end of this longest hockey season.

THE SEASON PRESENT

SHORTLY before the 1973 Stanley Cup playoffs began, Montreal Canadiens goalie Ken Dryden was asked about the New York Rangers' chances. "If the Rangers don't win The Cup this year," Dryden replied, "it probably will be a long time before they do."

Dryden was probably being more realistic than immodest. His answer was based on the vast roster of talent that belongs to the Montreal Canadiens, who won both The Prince of Wales Trophy and The Stanley Cup last Spring. Not only do the Canadiens boast such proven stars as Dryden, Jacques Laperriere, Guy Lapointe, Serge Savard, Yvan Cournoyer, and the Mahovlich Brothers, Peter and Frank, but they are oozing with talent on their farm teams, not to mention on the bench.

Behind Dryden were gifted young Michel Plasse and Wayne Thomas. On defense there was Larry Robinson and Pierre Bouchard, each of whom starred in the playoffs. And that was just starters. Youngsters such as goalie Bunny Larocque, center Dave Gardner, and wings Chuck Arnason and Yvon Lambert would be first-stringers on just about any other team in the NHL but had to wait on line until an opening developed on the Canadiens.

For that reason alone, the Flying Frenchmen are favored to finish first and retain The Stanley Cup in the Spring of 1974. "We have rebuilt, this time, in the last five years," said Canadiens managing director Sam Pollock, "and I think the future looks pretty solid."

If the Canadiens' future is solid, the Boston Bruins are shakier than they've been in five years. Nobody, least of all managing director Harry Sinden, can predict whether Phil Esposito or Bobby Orr will regain their old-time form. Esposito suffered a serious ligament injury against the Rangers last April and may never be the same. Orr had surgery on his knee during the Summer of 1972, but his moves last season suggested that he wasn't the pre-surgery Bobby Orr; and what's worse, may never be.

The team most likely to pass Boston and challenge the Canadiens is New York's Rangers. They have two first-rate goalies in Ed Giacomin and Gilles Villemure. Center Walt Tkaczuk is on the threshold of passing Esposito as the strongest center in the NHL; and defenseman Brad Park always seems about ready to reach Orr's level of excellence.

But the Rangers will have to contend with the Buffalo Sabres, an upstart expansion team which beat the Broadway Blueshirts five out of six times last year and should show even more poise this time around. A lot will depend on the development of promising youngsters such as defenseman Jim Schoenfeld and forward René Robert.

Starting with rookie coach Ted Garvin, Detroit's Red Wings will lean heavily on speedy little center Marcel Dionne, who scored 40 goals and 50 assists last season. "Guys bug me about my size," said Dionne, "but I'm smarter than them and don't get into fights with them. When a big guy calls me Froggy or Pipsqueak, I just tell him where to go and skate away as fast as I can."

As proven last Spring, Dionne can't do it alone for Detroit. He gets help from 52-goal Mickey Redmond, but not much more than that. Unless the Red Wings beef up their defense and obtain consistent goaltending, the playoffs will remain out of their reach.

The same can be said for the Toronto Maple Leafs, despite the hard work of center Dave Keon and wingers Ron Ellis and Paul Henderson. Despite first-rate goalies Doug Favell and Ed Johnston, the Leafs will have all they can do to fight off Vancouver and the New York Islanders in the race to stay out of the cellar.

Curiously, the Islanders, who lost 60 games last season, are in a splendid position to move up the ladder. They selected first in the junior draft and picked outstanding defenseman Denis Potvin, who will team up with his brother, Jean Potvin, on the Islanders back line. Bill Harris, who scored 28 goals as a rookie in 1972-73 figures to improve, while Gerry Desjardins gives the sophomore squad experienced and frequently outstanding goaltending.

Once again Chicago appears to be the class of the West

Division. In Stan Mikita, Dennis Hull, Jim Pappin, Pit Martin, and Cliff Koroll, the Black Hawks show mighty firepower. The addition of Dale Tallon will help at center, or defense, and Tony Esposito remains one of the best goalies in the league.

To finish second again, the Philadelphia Flyers will have to get another good year out of Bobby Clarke and another season of intimidation from such members of the "Mean Machine" as Dave Schultz, Don Saleski, Andre Dupont, and Bob Kelly.

As always, Minnesota's problem remains its aging legs. Dean Prentice, and Ted Harris can't go on forever, but Dennis Hextall, Jude Drouin, and Danny Grant may be the North Stars' salvation. Likewise, the St. Louis Blues must solve their goaltending woes and shore up their battered defense to keep ahead of Pittsburgh and Los Angeles, each of which gave them a run for fourth place last season.

Atlanta baffled everyone in 1972-73 with a near-playoff team. The Flames obtained extraordinary goaltending from Phil Myre and surprise scoring from center Curt Bennett, one of the most intelligent players in the game. "What's encouraging about Atlanta," said Bennett, son of a former NHL goaltender "is that most of the guys on the club read books when we travel. People who read tend to be less critical and tend to enjoy life more. Everybody needs an escape from hockey."

The Flames should at least escape the West Division cellar owned by the California Golden Seals. Except for goalie Gilles Meloche and freshman forward Hilliard Graves, the Seals have little to commend except the color of their jerseys.

Predicting the WHA race is a bit more difficult. The Blazers have moved from Philadelphia to Vancouver, Ottawa has moved to Toronto, and the New York Raiders are now the New York Golden Blades. But when all is said and done Winnipeg still has Bobby Hull, Cleveland has Gerry Cheevers, and the Whalers have the best balance overall. The leaders figure to be the same. After that, the positions are up for grabs.

SYL APPS, JR. "He reminds me of his old man."

That is the highest compliment any hockey fan could ever deliver to Syl Apps, Jr., the Pittsburgh Penguins center and son of the Toronto Maple Leafs' Hall Of Famer.

Former Penguins coach Red Kelly had played against the elder Apps and agreed that father and son have a lot in common. "Young Syl's dad was a great guy and a great player," said Kelly. "He went so fast I looked like a post on the ice by comparison. His son shows similar qualities. He's strong and he hits and he has a good fake. This is something that has to be born in a hockey player. It comes from breeding. Young Syl has the breeding, and I've always said that bloodlines are a wonderful thing."

But in Apps' case, breeding also means pressure—the onus of having to live up to your father's reputation. In Syl's case it was an awesome burden to bear.

"I used to feel pressures when I was growing up," said the tall, handsome Toronto native. "From kids' hockey right through my upper Junior days the fans would say that the only reason I was playing was because of my father's name. But you reach a point where, if you're not good enough, a name isn't going to win you a job. You have to do it on your own ability."

Syl, Jr., climbed from the Junior ranks to the Kingston Frontenacs Senior club and then to the New York Rangers' farm system. He played two games for Buffalo in the American League during 1968-69, scored one goal and two assists and promptly was given a "watch-carefully" tag by the New York scouts.

A season later he was transferred to Omaha of the Central Pro League and scored 16 goals and 38 assists for 54 points in 68 games. One scouting report described him thus: "Apps, Jr. is a splendid skater, a good puck-handler and playmaker, just like his father."

15

During the 1970 CHL playoffs he scored a league-leading ten goals and nine assists for 19 points in 12 games. He also played seven playoff games for Buffalo and managed a commendable two goals and three assists.

Always in the background was the awareness of his father's eminence in Canadian life. Syl, Sr., had become a member of the Ontario Legislature for Kingston and a member of the Cabinet.

"My father never pushed me in hockey," said Syl. "The only place he pushed me was in school. He always threatened to make me quit hockey if my marks slipped below 70. But I never did find out if he ever meant it."

The Rangers meant it when they promoted him to the big team in 1969-70; at least Syl, Jr., thought so. He started the season with New York but saw only occasional ice time and became more and more discouraged to the point of telling teammate Brad Park he wanted to quit hockey.

Syl, Jr., remembered: "At the time, the Rangers were fighting for first place and they didn't have much confidence in me. In that situation even one goal could make a difference and it was tough for them to use an inexperienced man."

When Syl was traded by the Rangers to Pittsburgh in January 1970 the Penguins' fans were not exactly delirious with joy. Pittsburgh general manager Jack Riley sent the popular—if not productive—Glen "Slats" Sather to New York. One irate Penguins fan hung a sign in the home rink: "WHY SLATS?" Obviously, Syl had a lot of work cut out for him.

Ironically, it was in a game against Toronto—his dad's former team—that Syl was architect on a goal that brought Penguins fans to his side. First he faked Ron Ellis and then dispatched a pass to teammate Greg Polis who went in for the score. Not long after that, Syl himself executed a breakaway goal which left then coach Red Kelly dancing in the aisles. To this day Kelly considers it a gem of offensive hockey.

"Jacques Plante was in the Toronto nets," Kelly recalled. "Syl first gave him a lunge to his right and then a lunge to his left. I could see Plante thinking 'I've got him' and put his stick out for the puck. But then Syl decked him again and it made bubbles inside me. It was the most beautiful goal I've seen in a long time."

Soon after that the "WHY SLATS?" sign came down. And Syl's scoring went up and up. Last season he led the Penguins in points with 29 goals and 56 assists for 85 points. Meanwhile Sather had scored 11 goals and 15 assists for 26 points, 54 less than Apps. Which proves that it was one of the most one-sided deals in National Hockey League history.

"I don't think anyone knew Syl would turn out to be such a fine hockey player," said Riley. "If Emile Francis knew then what he knows now he wouldn't have made the trade."

And it's a good thing, too, that young Apps made it, because he was entertaining thoughts about quitting hockey if he didn't catch on. "I decided to give it a try for three years," he admitted. "If I wasn't established I would have quit. I figured I didn't have much to lose. What's the difference if you get started in the business world when you're twenty-two or twenty-five?

"Fortunately, things broke right for me in Pittsburgh. I got more confidence and I'm carrying the puck a lot more. I'm learning when to hold it and when to let it go. I've got more finesse, too."

Ken Schinkel, who succeeded Kelly as coach during the 1972-73 season, admires Syl as much as anybody. "The thing he has going for him," said Schinkel, "is that he never stops. He has great determination to get the puck. If he thinks he has any kind of chance to get the puck, he'll go for it."

His hair flows long and he has the profile of, as Roy McHugh of *The Pittsburgh Press* put it, "a Victorian poet." They love him so much in Pittsburgh that Glen Sather couldn't come back if he paid his way on to the Penguins roster. Syl is, in fact, considered a superstar in Pittsburgh. When somebody asked Riley if he'd trade Apps for Bobby Clarke, the Philadelphia Flyers wonder boy, Riley said he'd have to think hard about it. His answer, finally, calmed quite a few Pittsburgh citizens.

"I'd have to stick with Syl," said Riley. "At least we know what we have."

And that is virtually a carbon copy of Syl, Sr.

GERRY CHEEVERS There are some goaltenders in big-league hockey who, if you ask them the time of day, or day of the month, or month of the year, will reply with the cautious air of an espionage agent, "Ummm, that's hard to say."

Perhaps their reluctance to make a commitment on any subject is understandable when one realizes that they are under constant bombardment for seven months a year and it is rather prudent for them to avoid controversy.

Gerry Cheevers of the Cleveland Crusaders is not among them.

Unlike most of his colleagues, Gerry Cheevers has a refreshing knack of telling it like it is and if the rest of the world doesn't like it, well, that's just tough on the rest of the world. Many years ago he developed a knack for doing the unlikely; a trait that reached a point of perfection during the Summer of 1972 when he walked out on the Boston Bruins after winning The Stanley Cup for them only months earlier and signing with Nick Mileti's team in the brand new World Hockey Association.

The move demonstrated several important aspects of modern hockey; to wit: Cheevers is one of the best goaltenders in the world; the Bruins suffered mightily without him; and Gerry showed some kind of spunk by gambling with the new circuit. When Cheevers returned to Boston Garden on 27 November 1972 with the Crusaders, the 9,000 spectators knew immediately that the Bruins would never be the same without the man they called "Cheesie." Veteran Boston hockey writer Tom Fitzgerald of *The Globe* observed: "Those who profess allegiance to the Bruins must have had cause for renewed regrets. They could hark back to Gerry's record of 32 unbeaten games (1971-72) as they marvelled at some of his clutch moves."

As expected, Gerry emerged as the best goalie in the WHA, if not the best in the world. Even members of the Boston Bruins, knowing that their overseers would be upset, allowed that Cheevers was top banana among the goaltenders during the 1972-73 campaign.

"He's the best in hockey today," said Derek Sanderson who, more than anyone, should know, since he played in both the WHA *and* the NHL during the 1972-73 season. "He'll win 1-0 or 10-9. He never gets uptight or mad at anyone. He always blames himself, not his defensemen. And he keeps his teammates loose."

NHL scoring champion Phil Esposito who knows all there is to know about goaltending is another Cheevers-booster. "With us," said Esposito, "Gerry was a winner. He used to tell me the average didn't matter, that he didn't care if we won 8-7. I didn't believe him. We'd talk about it and I'd say, 'C'mon, Gerry, admit it. You'd like a great average.' But he insisted that it didn't matter. After a while I believed him. I found out that he was one of the all-time greats when it came down to the money games."

Money was what lured Cheevers to the WHA. He received an estimated $1,000,000 deal to switch to Cleveland for seven years. It was double what the Bruins had to offer. "At first," Cheevers recalled, "I thought of 999 reasons why I should stay in Boston. Then I thought of 999 reasons why I should go. Reason number 1000 was the turning point: The money."

Those who thought Gerry wouldn't try as hard in the WHA didn't know the inner aspect of the man. "I've got pride," he said. "I get it out of winning. I've got pride in the WHA, for what we're trying to do and for what we had to overcome."

Make no mistake, there's also a light side to Gerry, one that frequently surfaces. Cheevers doesn't limit his exuberance to newsmen or to teammates. Once, a few years ago, he walked into a men's shop in Boston to buy himself some clothes. As Gerry tried on a jacket, a chap noticed that he was the Boston Bruins goaltender. He approached Cheevers.

"You've got the life," the man said. "You get a great salary and all you've got to do is stand in front of the net for two hours a night a couple of nights a week."

Gerry sized him up for a couple of seconds. "Tell you what," he replied, "I'll trade you jobs any day and we'll see how easy goaling really is."

Needless to say, the man declined. Cheevers then turned to a friend, "There's a saying among our fraternity that you have to be nuts to be a goaltender. The fact is, we're trained to do what we're doing and it's not all that impossible."

One reason why it's more possible for Cheevers than for other goaltenders is that he has several safety valves while his colleagues are more limited. For one thing, the thirty-three-year-old takes himself a little less seriously than other goalies. For another, he has an excellent outlet for his emotions in horse racing.

"I've been around the track for about fifteen years," he explained. "First it was Fort Erie, Ontario, then Woodbine, near Toronto. I like racing because of the people and the thoroughbred race horse. I think it's the greatest thing in the world."

Cheevers' interest in the track developed during his teenage days in his hometown of St. Catherines, Ontario. He met and befriended a horse trainer named Bob Warner; Gerry has been a racing fanatic ever since.

"Warner knew I was a junior goalie at the time," Gerry recalled, "and he loved hockey. He once explained to me that a stable was trained the way a hockey team was coached. That is, every horse is different and has to be treated that way.

"A young horse, like a rookie player, has to be worked hard and taught how to run. In other words you play hockey the way the manager wants you to play and you play sound hockey.

"A fat horse, he'd say, possibly referring to me because I tend to get overweight, has to be put in shape: like the long lengthy workouts in horseracing. The comparison with hockey is that a fat guy will get more pressure from the coach, and he'll have to do something extra on the ice after the workout."

During the non-hockey months, Cheevers does racing public relations and conducts interviews at the track. His mind is so organized that he now inevitably makes comparisons between hockey and racing.

"There are horses," he went on, "that have to be pampered the way some hockey players have to be babied. When I was playing minor league hockey in Rochester my coach was Joe Crozier. He was one of the best coaches I've ever played with and he had to pamper me.

"Then, you have the stake horses in racing and the stake horses in hockey. In hockey they're Bobby Hull and Phil Esposito. They'll run their own race. I don't think they can have any disturbance from the management or the coach.

"I've always felt that a thoroughbred always was worth studying. And race-trackers are the most down-to-earth, honest, and fair people I've ever met."

Gerry's infatuation with thoroughbred racing frequently intermingles with his love of fantasy. For several years he had nurtured an idea about authoring a first-person book, and then he wrote one. He had another idea according to Cheevers, the author (Gerry) would be a race horse on the morning of the Kentucky Derby. Action would zero in on his stall while the grooms attend to him.

"And then," said Gerry, transferring himself into the fictional role of the horse, "I start to look back over my career. How I started as a yearling in Kentucky and how no one thought I could make it. I'm not fashionably bred and I don't have too much style. But I start to win some races after a bad beginning and suddenly people aren't laughing anymore.

"I become a sensation, a real surprise. And here I am now at Churchill Downs, waiting for the big one . . ."

When someone asked him just how the story ends, Gerry winked, "To know that, you'll have to buy the book."

According to Gerry, he'll remain in hockey "until they stop issuing me pads at training camp," but his interest in racing will continue long after that.

"I've got a dream," he said. "It's something that comes up every two or three days of my life. I want to train a champion thoroughbred. Mind you, not own one, but train one. But that won't happen until hockey is finished.

"I'm not highstrung like a lot of other goalies," said Cheevers. "I consider myself carefree and that's one reason I avoid tension. But actually, I have deep thoughts on everything.

Including himself.

"As far as my own playing is concerned there's always some room for improvement. I have no set pattern of goaltending. I'm not a stand-up type and I'm not a flopper. I might do either one in a particular situation. I have a lot of confidence in my stick and my ability to skate.

"I always had hopes of being a Glenn Hall or a Jacques Plante. I've given myself enough years to reach these goals and I've never panicked. It takes time for a goaltender to develop; in our business, experience is the greatest thing in the world."

"I keep everything I learn on the opposition in my mind," Gerry said. "If I see a player shooting twice in the same place—to the top corner—I'll remember that and be sure to cover up the next time."

Cheevers' "book" on the opposition helped his roommate, rookie goalie Bob Whidden, who relieved Gerry from time to time in the Crusaders' nets last season. "Gerry," said Whidden, "would spend time with me. He'd tell me where the different players shoot—and it seemed that he was always right. Like he told me about J.C. Tremblay, how he would shoot high on my stick side. Sure enough, every time we played Quebec, that's where Tremblay shot the puck."

Perhaps the highest compliment one could pay Cheevers was delivered by Boston attorney Bob Woolf, who likened Cheevers to former basketball ace Bill Russell. "Except for Russell," said Woolf, himself a former crack basketeer, "I don't know any other athlete who got up for a game like Cheevers.

"He psychs himself to the degree that you feel nobody can touch him. And he believes this. He's an easy-going fellow who makes up his mind to do something—and then he goes ahead and does it, whatever it is."

It is something the Bruins discovered to their dismay and the Crusaders to their everlasting joy.

BOBBY CLARKE A few of his opponents may differ, but Bobby Clarke comes closest among the new National Hockey League aces to being the All-American—or All-Canadian—Boy. His gap-toothed grin; his effervescence; his determination to make the Philadelphia Flyers a winner have made him a hero among heroes not merely because he is an excellent player but because he plays the game very hard and as fairly as possible. On top of that, he's as modest as a fourth-stringer.

"Sure, I hear talk about being the next superstar," Clarke admitted, "but I generally ignore such stuff. I don't want to get myself thinking about that. First thing that would happen is that I'd start worrying about my image, and I don't think I could play the game under that kind of pressure."

But the pressure will be on this twenty-four-year-old center from Flin Flon, Manitoba, from now on; especially after what he did during the 1972-73 campaign. Playing in all 78 of his club's regular season games, Clarke finished second in the scoring race behind Boston's Phil Esposito. Bobby scored 37 goals and 67 assists for 104 points, and was the prime reason why the Flyers gained a playoff berth and reached the Stanley Cup semi-finals.

To the Flyers front office, Clarke was important in still another vital department—the battle between the World Hockey Association Blazers, led by Derek Sanderson in the Fall of 1972, and the Flyers, led by Clarke.

The fans came to see Bobby and stayed away from Derek. Eventually, Sanderson left the Blazers and returned to Boston. Still later the Blazers packed their bags and left Philadelphia. It was a clear-cut victory for the NHL over the WHA, but only because Clarke triumphed over Sanderson. And Bobby went on to win The Hart Trophy.

It was a gratifying victory for Bobby because when

Derek originally arrived in Philadelphia, Sanderson captured the attention of the media with such observations as "I'm a better hockey player than Clarke in certain phases of the game" and assorted other commentary that irritated Flyers' general manager Keith Allen more than it did Clarke.

"Derek and I have different life-styles," Clarke explained. "I'm very ordinary. I was raised that way, and I'm happy that way. I have a wife, a baby and a mortgage. My house has a small swimming pool, and I drive a Corvette. I don't enjoy making commercials and going to banquets, probably because I don't have enough self-confidence. Besides, I don't need any extra money. I'm making quite a bit more than I ever thought I'd make ($100,000 a year) and it's enough. I used to figure that if I was making $18,000 or $20,000 when I was twenty-three, I'd be doing great."

Clarke, who stands 5-10, 180 pounds, blossomed as a first-rate National Hockey Leaguer during the Team Canada-Russia series in September 1972. He was considered an effective forward when it started; but once the series had ended, Bobby was being talked of as one-two with Phil Esposito as the best center in the NHL.

"Those were pretty emotional games," Bobby flashed back. "Maybe the eight most important games hockey's ever had. When it was over, you felt like a season had ended, like you wanted to go someplace and play some golf."

That's precisely when the Flyers needed him most. Bobby returned to Philadelphia and helped take a team which, disappointingly, had missed the playoffs in the previous season, and converted them into a galvanic contender. In any given game, an observer could expect to see a classic of textbook hockey executed by Clarke. He did just that once in an 8-3 win over California, scoring two goals and an assist in an eight-minute flurry.

"Clarke looked like a spaniel romping amongst St. Bernards," wrote Stan Hochman in the *Philadelphia Daily News,* "frisking into corners, pouncing on the puck, sliding dart-like passes onto a teammate's stick. He played with a butterfly brilliance."

Remember, this young man is a diabetic, and was con-

sidered too much of a risk when he graduated from the
Flin Flon Bombers of the Western Canada (Junior)
League in the Spring of 1969. At the June amateur draft
that year the word was to avoid Clarke because of his
diabetes. As a result, he wasn't selected until the seven-
teenth selection; and this despite a brilliant career as a
junior.

Clarke has had an obsessive desire to keep diabetes out
of conversations about his rise to stardom. But it is impossible to avoid his accomplishment. Early in 1973 it was
acknowledged when he became general campaign chairman of the Delaware Valley Diabetes Association. What
will Clarke say about his conquest of his condition?

"I've proven that I can play in the NHL," he said. "In
the beginning if I didn't play well, I didn't want them
saying it was because of that [the diabetes]. Now, I've
proven I can play." His MVP selection proved that.

If you don't believe it, ask Derek Sanderson and the
chaps who had invested in the Philadelphia Blazers.

YVAN COURNOYER The deceptive aspect of Montreal
Canadiens right wing Yvan Cournoyer is that it appears
he can be intimidated out of scoring goals. He stands a
mere 5-7 and weighs only 165 pounds and has a soft,
pleasant face, suggesting the often pathetic 97-pound
weakling who was kicked around in the muscle-building
ads.

In the sixth and final game of the Stanley Cup finals between Montreal and the Chicago Black Hawks last May,
Jerry Korab, the behemoth who skated opposite Cournoyer for Chicago, tried to frighten Yvan with a verbal
uprising.

During a lull in the action, the 6-3, 205-pound Korab
stared down Cournoyer with his best bullying behavior

and sneered, "Hey, Shorty, what do you plan to do when you grow up?"

It wasn't the first time Yvan heard such derisive jibes and it certainly won't be the last. He immediately shot back at his tormentor, "I'm not sure. Score goals, I guess."

The score was tied 4-4 at the time. Montreal led the pulsating final round three games to two, but this sixth game was being played before a partisan Chicago Stadium crowd of more than 20,000. Early in the third period it appeared that the Black Hawks would break the game wide open in their favor. But they couldn't put the puck past Ken Dryden. It was then that Cournoyer, the thirty-year-old nicknamed "The Roadrunner," did his thing.

His thing is to emerge when he is least expected to emerge. Teammate Jacques Lemaire explained it precisely. "Even when his opponents skate with him," said Lemaire, "and very few guys can, Yvan is tough to cover because he shifts around so much. I've been playing beside him for years and even I lose track of him. One of his favorite tricks is to suddenly cut across from the right side to the center. If the man guarding him follows, the whole side of the rink they left is wide open and, poof, one of us scores."

And so it was, on that memorable night of 10 May 1973, when the Black Hawks thought they had the Canadiens on the run. Chicago's attack was blunted and Montreal launched into a counter-thrust. Lemaire skated over the Black Hawks' blue line and sent a high, hard shot that screamed over the net, bounced off the protective glass behind the goal, and richocheted back in front of the net, where goalie Tony Esposito was having difficulty following the disk.

With the special sense that the unique goal-scorers possess, Cournoyer burst away from his Chicago defenders. "Just when you think you have him tied up," said Black Hawks left wing John Marks, "he disappears on you." In a trice, Yvan surfaced directly behind the rebounding puck, about 20 feet in front of goalie Esposito. His arrival on that spot at that time amazed even veteran hockey critics.

"Just where Cournoyer came from hasn't been determined," said one press box observer. "It seemed as though a trap door had opened in the Stadium floor and he'd climbed up out of it just as the puck arrived in the area."

It would not be an easy shot for Yvan. The puck actually was in mid-air when he swung his stick, but he connected the way a good home run-hitter connects, and sent the rubber winging past the groping glove and pad of Esposito. The time was 8:13 of the third period. Montreal scored another goal to take the game, and The Cup, 6-4, but it was Yvan's score that won the game.

More than that, it won him a new automobile as the playoff's most valuable player and it won him a line in the NHL record book. Cournoyer had broken Frank Mahovlich's mark of 14 playoff goals with his game-winner, Yvan's 15th in the playoffs.

If any of the Black Hawks were wondering why the little guy couldn't be intimidated they might have consulted Cournoyer's teammates. They knew more than anyone that Yvan was skating through The Stanley Cup rounds with an agonizing stomach injury. His muscles had been strained earlier in the season, and for two months he was living with the discomfort.

"Don't make it sound like I'm a brave man," said Yvan when reporters questioned him about the problem during the finals. "It's just a little bit of pain that gets worse when I skate a lot. We have other guys playing with worse injuries. When it's the playoffs, you understand, it doesn't matter."

What amazed the Black Hawks was the fact that the injury failed to slow down Cournoyer by even one mile per hour. Yvan proved it in the fourth game of the series at Chicago—perhaps the most vital match of the series—which Montreal captured, 4-0.

Cournoyer's goal, the second of the game, came midway in the second period and was the crusher. It also was a thing of beauty, as teammate Lemaire pointed out. "Marc Tardif was forechecking," said Lemaire, "and he got the puck in the Chicago end. He put it back into the slot without looking too much because he knew what would happen. Yvan jumped in there and, boom, it was in the net."

That helps explain why Cournoyer scored 40 goals and 39 assists for 79 points, leading the Canadiens to The

Prince of Wales Trophy (for first place in the East Division). A season earlier he had 47 goals and 36 assists and, in 1970-71, 37 goals and 36 assists. Obviously, the man knows what scoring is all about.

What is rather unusual is his consistency under fire. Time and again, the hatchetmen among the enemy try to immobilize him with vicious spears, crosschecks, and other illegal forms of hockey warfare. "They hit me a lot in the final game we had in Chicago," Yvan remembered, "but that was all right. Some nights you need a bit of hitting to wake you up. Personally, I don't care too much about it."

The one thing Yvan has cared about since he was a kid growing up in the French-speaking town of Drummondville, Quebec, has been goals. When Cournoyer was 14 his family moved to Montreal and he quickly climbed hockey's sandlot ladder. Eventually he made it to Lachine, a powerful team in the Canadiens-sponsored Metropolitain Junior League.

NHL scouts had heard good things about the slick-haired kid with the big part in his hair but they really took notice after the final game of the Lachine-Verdun series. Yvan's club was trailing by one goal with less than a minute remaining in the deciding game when he captured the puck behind his own net. Bobbing and weaving, he skated past the opposition and shot the puck past the Verdun goalie. Then he scored the winning goal in sudden-death overtime.

Eventually Cournoyer graduated to the Junior Canadiens, a teen-aged but regal version of the parent club.

This was very fortunate for the Canadiens, who were scanning the junior hockey horizon for an eventual heir apparent to Henri Richard and Jean Beliveau, the reigning French-Canadian scoring titans. The *Habitants* called him up for a five-game tryout in the 1963-64 season and he scored in his very first game. "He pounces on the puck like a cat," said former Canadiens captain Beliveau.

Likening Yvan to a cat has an almost religious significance in Montreal. In all Canadiens history there was only one player who earned the nickname. That was Johnny "Black Cat" Gagnon, who twice led the team in scoring six and seven years before Cournoyer was born. Like

Yvan, Gagnon was a right winger. Soon they were calling Yvan "The Black Cat II."

Former Montreal coach Toe Blake was less enthused about Cournoyer than the phrase-makers. He gave Yvan only part-time work during his rookie year, 1964-65, and Cournoyer scored only seven goals. "But I never let down," says Yvan, "because when you let down you're finished. I said to myself eventually I would have my chance."

A season later he had scored 18 goals but still was used almost exclusively on the power play. By 1966-67 he was up to 25 goals but Blake remained critical of Yvan's defensive play. Then the coach decided to gamble and use him as a regular right wing and, amazingly, Cournoyer's defensive record immediately improved. "Toe kept harping at it," says Yvan, "and I kept working at it."

It was just as well that Blake put him on a line with Beliveau and hard-rock John Ferguson because the French-speaking clientele at The Forum had become impatient with the coach.

"On veut Cournoyer" (we want Cournoyer) was a standard chant when Yvan wasn't on the ice and the demands increased as his goal total climbed. He reached 28 in 1967-68 and on 12 March 1969 he scored his fortieth goal of the 1968-69 season. With eight games left in the schedule it was almost possible for Yvan to reach the 50-goal plateau. But he only scored three more and actually felt relieved about the whole thing.

"If I decided that I had to score fifty," he says, "everytime I missed a goal I should have scored I'd have brooded over it. That's no good. If you keep brooding you stop getting your chances."

The record indicates that Yvan has had little time to brood. In eight full seasons as a Canadien he has played on six Stanley Cup winners. But he never was more a part of the world champion machine than on that night last May when he embraced The Stanley Cup in Montreal's dressing room and shouted, "Yoooo-hooooo!! This is a night I can't ever forget."

To a man, the Montrealers agreed that little Yvan deserved all the applause—and money—he received. Huge Peter Mahovlich, who appreciated the word of the smaller

men as much as anyone on the Canadiens summed up
what the hockey world felt about Yvan.

"Cournoyer and Henri Richard are the greatest guys in
the world," said Mahovlich. "They're cut from the same
mold."

The label on the mold reads—"clutch player."

KEN DRYDEN The best goaltender in the National
Hockey League?

There are several good ones; Roger Crozier of Buffalo,
Ed Giacomin and Gilles Villemure of the Rangers, and
Tony Esposito of Chicago.

But the man who won The Vezina Trophy in 1972-73
and led the Montreal Canadiens to first place in the East
(The Prince Of Wales Trophy) and The Stanley Cup was
none other than lawyer-goaltender Ken Dryden.

The professorial twenty-six-year-old Dryden played in
54 regular season games for a 2.26 goals against average,
topping Villemure (2.29), Esposito (2.51), and Roy Edwards of Detroit (2.63) among the top four. And Ken
tied Edwards for the shutout lead with six.

All in all 1972-73 was a remarkable season for Dryden,
who actually began playing in August 1972 when he
launched training for the fabled Team Canada-Russia
series in which he played a prominent part. "The last season was so long," Ken recently observed, "that I can't
remember when I wasn't playing."

The opposition does remember. An aching back sidelined Dryden late in January 1973 and through the
following month, with what often appears to be a chronic
problem with Ken. He suffered a similar ailment the previous year. "For a few games after I returned in 1971-72,"
Ken said, "I wondered if the condition might recur, but
after a while I forgot about it entirely. And then it cropped
up again."

The hospitalization late last Winter was a tonic in more ways than one; it enabled Ken to return and pace the Canadiens to the pennant and it gave him time to relax and reflect. It also provided his hospital roommate, an old sculler named Buster Thom, the opportunity to gain some rare up-close insights into Dryden not available to the average fan.

"I'll tell you something about Ken," Thom revealed, "he has the virtue of infinite patience. When he was in that room the telephone rang at least 75 times a day, but Ken treated every single caller as courteously as the next."

Many of Dryden's teammates and colleagues have been known to be considerably more abrupt and occasionally hostile with the man-in-the-street. How did Ken account for his easy-going attitude toward the fans?

"I enjoy the calls," he explained. "The kids who phone usually start off by stuttering a little when you say something. It's nice to hear from them, and when you're in the hospital with nothing to do, it helps your morale.

"It reminded me of the time when I was a kid and my hero was a pitcher on the Toronto Maple Leafs of the International League. His name was Steve Ridzik. One day I went up to him and asked for his autograph. He gave me the Alvin Dark treatment—'take a hike, kid'—and walked off with a case of twenty-four under his arm. What a letdown that was for me."

Dryden never let his fans down when he returned to the Canadiens' lineup, but some of his opponents quietly wished he had stayed in the hospital last March—the Detroit Red Wings in particular.

Locked in a playoff drive with the Buffalo Sabres, the Red Wings went up against Montreal at The Forum on 10 March 1973 and left the ice babbling to themselves after Ken had beaten them, 2-0.

Those Detroiters who were the most upset were Marcel Dionne (clear breakaway), Bill Collins (missed a clear shot from the side), Mickey Redmond (seven good chances), Al Karlander (clean breakaway), Red Berenson (missed rebound), and Ron Stackhouse (bounced shot off goalpost). "We played our best game of the year," said then Detroit coach Johnny Wilson, "and what does Dryden give us, nothing!"

In all fairness, Detroit wasn't the only team to receive such treatment. Ken applied his wizardry wherever he travelled and against whomever he faced on any given night. Once last March, against the Toronto Maple Leafs, Dryden showed what superior goaltending is all about. It's like outstanding pitching in baseball. The team behind the goalie—or pitcher—can play a mediocre game but the first-rate goalie or pitcher can somehow manage to pull off a win. On that March night the Leafs completely dominated the Canadiens at The Forum and ex-Montreal captain Jean Beliveau walked out of the rink singing the highest praises for his former teammate.

"Goaltending is the secret of success in hockey," said Beliveau, "and we had an example of that when Dryden came from nowhere to take Ron Ellis' shot out of the air with one hand when it appeared to be going into the open net in the third period. He has tremendous coordination, speed, and reflex action for such a big [6-4, 210] man."

Montreal won the game, 4-1. To those in the audience there was more than ordinary symbolism in the events on ice. "That team [Montreal] will win The Stanley Cup because they have Ken Dryden in goal," said Maple Leafs vice president King Clancy. "He's as good as any other goalkeeper I've ever seen. Like all the great ones, he makes the seemingly impossible saves."

Clancy was right. Montreal beat Buffalo, Philadelphia, and Chicago to capture The Cup—the second for Ken in three seasons. However, it was the first time he ever faced his older brother, Dave, in a Stanley Cup match. Dave, 32, guarded the twines for Buffalo in the opening game of the first round last April and played splendidly, although Ken beat him, 2-1.

"Dave played well," said Ken. "He always plays well against us. He frustrated us for the first 30 minutes of the game. It was just a matter of two really good shots beating him."

The younger Dryden was less than sensational in the finals against Chicago; but even when he's just good, it's very, very good, compared to most other goaltenders. A major asset in Ken's repertoire is his easy-going disposition. He knows how to relax.

His characteristic pose during lulls in the on-ice action—resting his chin on the top of his gloves and his gloves on the top of his stick—suggests Dryden's easy-going outlook. Naturally, he has other ways of relieving tension.

"Tennis," Ken said, "is wonderful. It removes a whole set of worries about hockey for a whole new set about tennis. For instance, has anyone got a cure for an erratic backhand or a balky serve?"

Dryden's diversions are numerous and almost legendary, especially his work with consumer advocate Ralph Nader in Washington, D.C. "Nader," said Ken, "is a lawyer with a conscience, and there aren't enough of that kind. He has an amazing grasp of many situations and the ability to relate to them. He knows where and how pressure should be exerted to do the most good. I learned from him that one man—you or I—can make a big difference in a bureaucracy."

Likewise, Nader has come to appreciate Dryden and his craft. Ralph visited Montreal once and saw Ken in action at The Forum. Nader came away convinced that the goaltender is as much a thorn in the side of the enemy as he is a pain in the neck of Washington's business establishment.

PHIL ESPOSITO Up until the night of 5 April 1973, the world was Phil Esposito's oyster. The tall Boston Bruins center had only a few days earlier been officially proclaimed the National Hockey League's leading scorer for the third straight year. His 55 goals and 75 assists for 130 points frequently were game-winners or game-tiers, and he was poised to direct the Bruins to a second consecutive Stanley Cup.

It wouldn't be easy; but, then again, it shouldn't be too hard, the experts thought. Boston first had to conquer the New York Rangers, a club they whipped in six games during the 1972 finals. Nobody worried that much about New

York. The Bruins had whipped the Rangers in the home-stretch of the 1972-73 race to land in second place, ahead of the Broadway Blueshirts.

The playoffs opened on Boston Garden ice and suddenly strange things happened. New York won the opening game, 6-2. Even worse, the line of Esposito, Ken Hodge and Wayne Cashman managed only two shots on New York goalie Ed Giacomin. Still more embarrassing, Esposito's opposite center, Walt Tkaczuk, scored two big goals for the Rangers.

Bruins fans dutifully hoped that the disaster was nothing more than a temporary aberration that would disappear when the teams met again for the second match at Boston Garden. As things developed, the Boston sextet didn't know what real trouble was until the second game.

Once again the Rangers were superior, winning the contest, 4-2, but the real trouble took place just inside the New York blue line when Esposito headmanned a Boston attack. The 6-1, 205-pound Bruin was being pursued by Rangers rookie Steve Vickers, who steered Phil toward hardrock defenseman Ron Harris.

Normally, Esposito's radar would have picked up Harris and Phil would have swerved out of danger. But the Rangers seemed to come from out of nowhere. "I backed into him with my hip coming from the other way," said Harris. "Before I got to him Vickers must have knocked him off-balance, and as he was going down I got him with the hip. It wasn't a dirty check."

Esposito crumpled to the ice, grimacing with pain. He had suffered torn medial collateral ligaments of the right knee and had to be carried from the ice. He was through for the season, and the Bruins were in deep, deep trouble.

"You can't measure the loss of the best player in hockey," said Phil's teammate Bobby Orr. "It doesn't look good for us."

That was clear as the Bruins were bounced out of the playoffs in five games. But of greater concern is the future of Esposito, because as Phil goes, so go the Bruins. Following his hospitalization, Phil wore a fourteen-pound cast to protect the ligament surgery on his right knee. Immediately, the dismal rumors started flying and Phil had all to do to shoot them down.

"Somebody told me that it was written that I'd have to play defense instead of center during the 1973-74 season," said Esposito. "That's ridiculous. In the first place, my knee is going to be 100 per cent; just as good as ever. Maybe at the beginning I'll be a little weak, but I'll get stronger. Being inactive all Summer has to take its toll." And therein lies the most vexing question of Esposito's glorious career; can Phil completely recapture the form that enabled him to so thoroughly dominate the scoring lists since he first won the Art Ross Trophy in 1969?

If Esposito has lost any of his touch, the Bruins will suffer terribly, as demonstrated during the 1973 playoffs. The success of Orr is intertwined with the presence of Esposito.

"Esposito and Orr have run the Bruins offense," said Bobby Hull who had played against them so long before he switched to the World Hockey Association. "Orr creates the situation and Esposito puts it away. They work perfectly together. They know that when one of them has the puck something is going to happen."

Ironically, Phil had enjoyed his headiest hockey moments even before the 1972-73 season began. More than any single player, he steered Team Canada to its stirring series triumph over the Russian National Team in September 1972, and was acclaimed as the super clutch player of the NHL.

He lost none of his touch during the regular season, although his point production was less than either of the two previous seasons. Still, despite a severe back injury to linemate Cashman and other internal team troubles, Phil moved to the top of the scoring pack and fought off a late season challenge from young Bobby Clarke of the Philadelphia Flyers. When the final figures were in, Esposito won the Ross Trophy going away—a big 26 points ahead of Clarke.

But that became old business as soon as the playoff began. Phil couldn't seem to get untracked against the persistent Rangers' checking—and then along came the explosive bodycheck by Harris.

As Esposito was being taken to the hospital, coach Bep Guidolin glumly remarked: "The coffin is still open; it's not closed yet. But they're getting the hammer and nails ready."

Should the Phil Esposito of 1973-74 be less than the player he was before the injury, Guidolin's quote might as well be dusted off and resurrected again for this season.

KEN HODGE With 12:22 remaining and the score tied 2-2 in the fifth game of the 1972 quarter-final Stanley Cup playoff series between the Boston Bruins and the Toronto Maple Leafs, Bruins' right wing Ken Hodge took a feed from linemate Phil Esposito in front of the Toronto cage. As Leafs' goaltender Bernie Parent slid, a trifle tardy, across the goal crease, the opportunistic Hodge banged the puck under Parent's right leather pad and the Bruins, who led the series three games to one, commandeered the comfortable side of what proved to be a final 3-2 score. So much for the quarter-finals.

"All I can say," the amiable but rough Hodge sighed in the dressing room after the contest, "is that this is a gratifying wind-up to a pretty horrible year."

Although the Bruins still had a chunk of season left to play on the way to their second Stanley Cup in three years, "horrible" is a fair description of Ken Hodge's 1971-72 experience in Boston.

"I was in an awful slump early in the season for a variety of reasons," the soft-spoken forward recalled. "I went something like 13 games without scoring. The fans in Boston Garden got on me pretty fiercely—deservedly so, too, I thought, because I was playing terribly.

"Then trade rumors began to appear in the papers—again," Hodge continued. "I tried not to get discouraged, but I was really pretty low."

Ever since Ken scored 45 goals during the 1968-69 season, the fans and the press have been yelling, "Encore!" But such feats are difficult to duplicate, unless you happen to be blessed with the puck sense of a Phil Esposito or Bobby Orr.

Nevertheless, the 6-2 215-pounder exceeded all expectations when he contributed 105 points to the Bruins' record-breaking 1970-71 campaign, only to be throttled in the playoffs by the super-psyched Montreal Canadiens.

Entering the 1971-72 season, Hodge and his mates were determined to dispel the bitter taste of that stunning upset. Former coach Tom Johnson laid down the law—defense would be the order of the season. It was as if the team was preparing for the playoffs from the outset of the campaign.

Stressing back-checking and other fundamentals makes goalies and defensemen happy, but if you're a big strong right winger with a booming slapshot and a heavy wrist shot, you naturally prefer a more "wide-open" style of play. Ken found it difficult to meld his offensive talents with the team's renewed endeavour for vigilance behind the blue line, and although he worked hard to sharpen his defensive skills, he began to sputter in both phases of the game. His name was mentioned in all sorts of imaginary deals—to California for a goaltender, to Chicago for a defenseman, to Toronto for a more disciplined right wing.

In the end, Hodge went to none of these places, but rather was summoned for a heart-to-heart talk with then Bruins' general manager Milt Schmidt. It was Schmidt, once a high-scoring center himself, who had engineered the most one-sided trade in hockey history, acquiring Hodge, along with pivot-men Phil Esposito and Fred Stanfield, for brawny defenseman Gilles Marotte, diligent center Pit Martin, and a mediocre netminder named Jack Norris. Schmidt wasn't about to tarnish his image as a wheeler-dealer by dumping Hodge as a dud. Instead, he sympathized with Kenny's plight, and assured the grateful right wing that he was in Boston to stay, at least for a while.

With the pressure off, Hodge's play showed immediate improvement.

"I got a few breaks here and there," he related. "Some goals went in. I was out of it all of a sudden."

Then, if you'll pardon the pun, Ken suffered his most unfortunate "break" of the season. Against the Minnesota

North Stars, the English-born Hodge swooped down upon the Minnesota cage and attempted to screen goalie Cesare Maniago from the play in front of the net.

When it comes to uninvited visitors in the goal crease, Cesare can be a most ungracious host. He took a mighty swipe at Hodge's ankle with his heavy goalie stick, and the Boston forward limped to the bench with a broken ankle.

What followed was six weeks of uncertainty for Ken. He spent a few weeks in Florida just taking it easy, when it suddenly dawned on him that maybe he had been carrying too much weight.

"I came to the conclusion that I was too heavy for my own good," Hodge reported. "So I took off 25 pounds while I was in Florida. I just quit eating bread and potatoes and pastry and it disappeared by magic."

When he returned to action later in the season, Ken weighed in at a slim 205 pounds and picked up where he had left off. He contributed mightily to the Bruins' thrust for The Stanley Cup, netting nine goals and eight assists in post-season play.

During the 1972-73 season, Ken seemed to reach an equilibrium point—somewhere between his best and worst seasons. He tallied 37 goals and 44 assists, despite missing five games due to a bruised wrist. Coach Bep Guidolin didn't hesitate to use Hodge in specialized situations and the stocky skater couldn't have been happier.

"Now I've got a position on the power play," he said, "and at odd times I'm used to kill penalties. It means more responsibility and I'm really glad it worked out this way."

So are the Bruins.

BOBBY HULL There are many reasons why the World Hockey Association survived its first season and was healthy enough to challenge the National Hockey League for the attention of fans after so short a time. The WHA had capable leadership. It benefitted from NHL carelessness and haughtiness and it boasted novelty value.

All of these and other reasons are valid, but the fact remains that the WHA succeeded for one reason above all—left wing Robert Marvin "Bobby" Hull. When, in June 1972, The Golden Jet signed a $2,750,000 ten-year contract with the Winnipeg Jets the WHA was made, because it now had a superstar, and that superstar more than any other gave the new league credibility.

A year before he switched leagues, Hull became only the second player in history to score more than 600 goals in the NHL, putting him at a career total of 604. Only Gordie Howe of the Detroit Red Wings topped that with 786 in his twenty-five NHL seasons.

The Golden Jet led the NHL in goal-scoring seven times and three times was point leader. He was named to the All-Star Team in twelve out of fifteen seasons and he had won just about every available award, including the Lady Byng Trophy for good sportsmanship combined with ability. At the age of thirty-four, when he put on the Winnipeg Jets uniform for the first time, Bobby Hull had done just about everything that had been asked of him; but now he was facing the biggest challenge of his life.

Curiously, his first challenge was maintaining his mental stability. In its desperate attempt to kill the WHA, the NHL attempted to bar Hull from playing by using every legal method at their command. A court injunction sidelined him for the first month of the campaign until, finally, that restriction was lifted, and once again The Golden Jet set turnstiles clicking as he had before.

And once again the red lights went on when Bobby shot and the crowds cheered; but it wasn't easy for him in those first weeks of his WHA debut. "I got awfully run down from all the litigation," Bobby admitted. "I lost more than ten pounds, down from 194 to 180, and since I don't carry any fat, that loss was all in muscle and red meat. I felt just plain unhealthy."

But he never stopped smiling and he never stopped providing the new league with that beautiful new, positive image that it needed so badly at the start. Bobby took an instant pride in the new league but he is the first to admit he left the Chicago Black Hawks for reasons other than building the WHA.

"If I told you that the big contract had nothing to do with my signing with Winnipeg," Hull smiled, "I'd be telling you a lie. It made the future secure for my family. That was the most important thing. Then there were some things that disenchanted me in the NHL, and the way the Hawks handled their attempts to sign me. They just didn't think I'd consider jumping."

Hull moved his wife, Joanne, and their five children into a fourteen-room $185,000 home in the Winnipeg suburb of Tuxedo. Natives of the Manitoba metropolis appropriately greeted him as a national hero and Bobby repaid them by taking the Jets right up to the top of the WHA's Western Division, which is where they finished.

The Jet scored 51 goals and 52 assists in 63 games to finish in a three-way tie for fourth place in the WHA scoring list with Tom Webster of New England and Winnipeg's Norm Beaudin. However, Webster played in 77 games and Beaudin in 78. Bobby's point total was amazing, considering that he frequently was skating at less than top speed.

"I never had many injuries until last season," he explained, "but every part of me seemed to hurt after I started skating for the Jets—my elbow, my shoulder and my knee. It was part of the complete changeover in the schedule. For fifteen years in the NHL we had three games a week with two days off after each game. In the first year of the WHA we had doubleheaders and back-to-back games, which meant that my little injuries never got a chance to heal."

Still, he was able to take Winnipeg all the way to the finals of the WHA's playoff for the Avco World Cup, before New England defeated the Jets four games to one. People who had never seen him before marvelled at the job he had done and extolled his performances despite all the legal problems.

During one of Hull's visits to Los Angeles, Bobby dazzled the hometown Sharks with his footwork and stickwork. "When does he ever take a rest?" asked Sharks goalie George Gardner. "Every time I looked up, there he was."

Winnipeg won the game, 6-5, in sudden death overtime. The home team had lost, but those who appreciate quality, such as *Los Angeles Times* reporter Dwight Chapin, waxed ecstatic over The Golden Jet.

"Hull did everything," said Chapin. "He scored twice. He added two assists. He was in on power plays. He killed penalties. He talked to his team, and argued moderately with officials.

"It was more or less a $3,500,000 performance."

That's why Bobby Hull made the WHA.

RICK MACLEISH There are people, I guess, who will look at Rick MacLeish's 1972-73 arithmetic and, with a cynical smirk, go on to expound on the utter cheapness of a big-league hockey goal, the evils of expansion, the dilution of talent, and then, with a glazed expression in their eyes, reflect on how "they just don't make hockey players like they used to."

Maybe so, but with 50 goals and 50 assists in his first full season in the National Hockey League, MacLeish deserves something more than just that negative whining.

Whether or not the Philadelphia Flyers ace will go on to establish himself as a consistent 50- or even 40-goal scorer, no one can really tell. But on the basis of this twenty-three-year-old's determination, one can only say that if he wants to, he will.

A quiet, reserved athlete off the ice, MacLeish had his problems before finally arriving as a legitimate scoring threat in the bigs. Drafted fourth by the Boston Bruins in the amatuer selections in 1970, Rick, then a left winger, was buried deep in the Boston organization. The Bruins had, of course, John Bucyk as their number one left winger with Wayne Cashman and Don Marcotte also playing the port side. No matter how good you are, that is competition.

"Boston felt I ought to be a left wing, same as in junior hockey and they kept telling me the opening would be there when Bucyk retired," MacLeish said. "Well, it's been several years since then and he's still going strong."

The next season, MacLeish and Ron Schock were traded to the Philadelphia Flyers for Mike Walton. But MacLeish had difficulty adjusting to the NHL and his new environment. After 17 games with the Flyers and only one goal produced, Rick was farmed to Richmond. The blow to his ego was crushing.

"I didn't have much desire for a while," Rick admitted. The quiet, sensitive MacLeish also found it a problem to adjust to Richmond's vitriolic coach Eddie Bush. "He knew his hockey, but I guess he didn't know how to tell it to the players," Rick recalled with dismay.

Flyers assistant coach, Mike Nykoluk, a former Hershey forward, remembered MacLeish. "He reminded me of a player who just had a shot. He looked like he had no desire to play, but I guess if you're sort of a reserved person, Eddie Bush is tough," Nykoluk said. "He is the kind that hollers and screams, and it can drive you into a shell."

After that disastrous season, MacLeish came to the Flyers' 1972 training camp ready to prove himself. Bobby Clarke was the talk of Philadelphia on the strength of his superb performance with Team Canada against the Russian National Team. The word around the Flyers' camp was that Bill Clement, a hustling young pivot, would be the Philadelphians' second center.

"That sort of made me play harder," MacLeish said.

What happened next is Rick's happy history. MacLeish, not Clement, became the second center and there were some who rated Rick higher than that. He finished the season as the NHL's fourth leading scorer behind Phil Esposito, teammate Clarke, and Bobby Orr. He notched an even 100 points on an equal number of goals and assists and led the entire league in power play goals with 21.

"I never dreamed of that kind of a year," Rick confided. "I set my sights on 20 goals and I thought that that might be stretching it."

MacLeish believes that much of his success is due to two major factors, the first being his release from the Boston organization and the second his being placed on a line with Gary Dornhoefer and Ross Lonsberry. On the power play, Rick centered for Cowboy Bill Flett and for Clarke.

The Flyers organization was patient with young Mac-Leish, and now that patience is paying off. "I guess a lot of people thought he would produce immediately," says Flyers general manager Keith Allen. "That trade put a lot of pressure on him. I don't doubt now that he is one of the best young centers in the league."

"He may have the fastest wrist shot in the league," boasts assistant coach, Mike Nykoluk. Flyers' GM Allen doesn't hedge at all on this subject. "He has the best wrist shot in the league," he inisists.

MacLeish's wrist shot has been a point of conversation around Philly for two seasons, and for good reason. A scorer of fifty goals who virtually disdains the slap, Mac-Leish talks about the wrist shot almost as much as he uses it.

"When I shifted to center, my old junior coach Roger Neilson told me to forget the slap shot and I have, completely. Even when we line up to practice shots from the blue line I work only with the wrist shot. I seem to have the ability to get it away quickly in the slot and that's where most of the goals have been coming from.

"You can do a lot more things with a wrist shot," Mac-Leish concluded. "You have a much better idea where the puck is going. Sometimes you can wind up and fake it, too, if there's time, and get the goalie moving out of position."

MacLeish's success at center has sparked confidence. Not only in himself but in his entire team. The Flyers' power play statistics speak for themselves in that department.

"The thing I like about playing center is the freedom it gives me to move around," he says. "The success of our power play has helped our confidence all around this year and has put us in the position of being a really close-knit team."

The Flyers' league-leading power play brought the Flyers to a second place finish in the West Division last season. After a hard-fought quarter-final round with the Minnesota North Stars, in which Rick scored two goals, the Flyers eliminated the Stars and moved on to the semis to face the red-hot Montreal Canadiens.

MacLeish's air of confidence was not dampened by the awesome prospect of facing the Frenchmen.

"We go into games in a confident mood now," MacLeish revealed, "and that's the way we seem to be coming into Montreal. We've done well against the Canadiens this year and I think we can beat them."

Youthful enthusiasm, right? Well, MacLeish showed that it was more than just that. In the first game of the semi-final series at the historic Montreal Forum, both teams were tied 2-2 at the end of regulation time. Early into the overtime period, a backchecking MacLeish stole a clearing pass from Frank Mahovlich, bore down on Ken Dryden and whipped his wrist shot past Dryden's lunging pads for the winning goal and a 1-0 edge in the series.

As it turned out, that was to be MacLeish's and Philadelphia's last moment in the sun for the season. Montreal methodically wore down the Flyers with experience and superior personnel, but MacLeish had received his baptism of fire.

"It was just a matter of gaining his confidence," says coach Nykoluk of MacLeish. "He isn't a kid anymore. Now he's a man."

FRANK MAHOVLICH It was the first day of Spring 1973 in Montreal; but hockey fans in that Quebec metropolis kept alluding to the Winter of Frank Mahovlich's life and the two nervous breakdowns he suffered earlier in his National Hockey League career. In fact, the same theme seemed to run all across Canada.

"FRANK MAHOVLICH," shouted a headline in *The Vancouver Sun*, "PRESSURE HIS WAY OF LIFE."

There were good reasons for the headlines and the spotlight on the Montreal Canadiens' gifted left wing. He had

scored 499 goals up until that day and was on the lip of a
milestone. On the all-time scoring parade the man they
call "Big M" was behind only Gordie Howe (786), Bobby
Hull (604), Maurice Richard (544), and Jean Beliveau
(507). Once again the pressure was on Frank and he was
the first to admit it.

"There's pressure," he said, "no matter where you play.
A lot of players try to avoid it but I think the important
factor is the way a man handles it."

Mahovlich has handled it in various ways at various
times. Since being traded from the Toronto Maple Leafs—
first to Detroit and then Montreal—Frank has become
more and more relaxed and consistently productive. In 78
regular season games last season, he scored 38 goals and
55 assists for 93 points to tie for seventh place in the scoring race. Helping the Canadiens to a second Stanley Cup
in three years, Mahovlich played in 17 playoff games and
scored nine goals and 14 assists for 23 points.

On that Spring night in Montreal, the Big M did score
his 500th goal and was hailed from the Maritimes to Brit-
ish Columbia for his accomplishment. "The key word
about the 500th goal," said *Montreal Star* sports editor
Red Fisher, "is greatness. Mahovlich has it." Yet to those
who have known him well it is hard to believe he has broken free from his black moments of the past. They recall
that during 1964-65 Frank's scoring slipped and he was
continuously booed on home ice when he played for
Toronto. Finally, he suffered the first of what were later
revealed to be nervous breakdowns, described as "deep
depression and tension."

"If Toronto fans would appreciate his great talent and
give him the cheers he deserves, instead of booing him,
maybe the pressure wouldn't cook the guy," said Red
Wing great Gordie Howe at the time.

But by then everyone knew that Frank Mahovlich was
peculiar, different from the average hockey player—even
his teammates couldn't understand the woeful-eyed
winger.

"I played with Frank for eleven years," ex-teammate Bob
Baun said, "and I probably never said twenty-two words
to the guy."

Pete Stemkowski, a former Toronto colleague, echoed Baun's sentiment:

"When we were in Toronto, you were lucky to get a hello from Frank."

Eventually Mahovlich returned to the Maple Leafs' lineup and to relative obscurity. That was another curious facet of The Big M's life—when he wasn't the best or the most disappointing or the sickest, he was virtually ignored by the press.

But the misunderstanding was to crop up again, ultimately leading to Frank's third "comeback."

In the middle of the 1967-68 season Mahovlich played an "outstanding" game, according to his supreme judge and arch critic, Toronto's manager-coach Punch Imlach. The Leafs beat the Canadiens, 5-0, at Maple Leaf Gardens, and Frank's goal and two assists earned him "second star" category by broadcaster Foster Hewitt after the game.

Frank skated out on the ice when his name was called, no doubt expecting the normal round of applause. But there was scant applause. Instead, he was greeted with a vocal round of jeering and hooting from season ticket holders who had long ago decided that no matter what Big M did, it wasn't good enough.

Frank left the ice, his perpetually sad face set and motionless. After changing in silence, he went to the sleeping car that would carry the team to Detroit, and sat brooding. At 4 o'clock in the morning he arose, found the team physician, and was escorted to a hospital. Frank once more was reported to be suffering from "deep depression and tension," and was in the care of a psychiatrist, Dr. Allan Walters.

It was obvious by this time that Toronto bigwigs, primarily Imlach, would love to unload the problematic Mahovlich, but he had to play again and prove he was worth a trade. Frank did return, with improvement.

Early in March of 1968 Imlach found his buyer, and manipulated one of hockey's most spectacular trades. Mahovlich, Stemkowski, and rookie Garry Unger—plus the rights to then-retired defenseman Carl Brewer—would go to Detroit for high-scoring Norm Ullman, Floyd Smith, and

talented young Paul Henderson. There were heated debates
as to which team had gotten the better of the trade.

Red Fisher believed that Detroit had the edge, but naturally not because of Mahovlich: "This is a man of superior
talent," said Fisher of the Big M, "but he is a disturbed
and fretful character. The most valuable acquisition in the
trade is Brewer."

And Punch made it painfully clear he was delighted to
be rid of his troublesome left wing. "Hockey is mostly a
streetcar named Desire. Sometimes Frank doesn't catch
it."

Frank appeared at first to be a rusty streetcar in Detroit, but it was near the end of the season and he merely
needed time to make his third NHL "comeback."

"It took about six months for me to get adjusted," he
said. "You know, they'd heard all the Frank Mahovlich
stories and they were wondering if they were true. And I
was never the kind of guy who tried to sell myself."

Bill Gadsby, a former NHL defenseman who had
played against Mahovlich, was named Detroit coach in
1968-69, and in a wise move, placed Frank at left wing on
the great Howe-Delvecchio line.

Right away the unit hit it off spectacularly. By March
of 1969 the line was tops in league scoring, and Frank finished among the top 10 with 49 goals and 29 assists for 78
points. His performance was almost as good the next year,
with 70 points. Frank was loose and happy, trading jokes
and banter with his teammates. And Detroit loved him. It
looked as though the bad days were all over.

But 1970-71 was bad, very bad for Detroit. The club
was torn by dissension, and in January 1971 Frank was
traded to Montreal in exchange for Mickey Redmond,
Guy Charron, and Bill Collins. Since then the Canadiens
have captured two Stanley Cups and the Red Wings none,
but both Montreal manager Sam Pollock and Detroit
manager Ned Harkness are satisfied with the deal.

"We needed a superstar to stabilize the team," said Pollock. "Ken Dryden was not with us yet and we were losing Jean Beliveau and John Ferguson. In Frank's case we
have a superstar for years to come."

In 1971 Frank scored a record 14 goals in the playoffs
to help decimate the Chicago Black Hawks. The mark last-

ed until the spring of 1973 when teammate Yvan Cournoyer lit 15 red lights. But fans still remember the big goal Frank scored in the sixth and final game against Chicago, when he outmuscled defenseman Pat Stapleton to jam the puck past goalie Tony Esposito and give Montreal the needed cushion.

Nobody deserved The Cup champagne any more than the Big M and nobody appreciated his genuine grin more than *Toronto Daily Star* reporter Red Burnett who remembered Frank when he suffered with Imlach and the Maple Leafs.

"The Big M," said Burnett, "has gone from a hockey robot to a happy, well-adjusted human being." So happy that he'd like to play hockey forever.

"I haven't given retirement any consideration," Frank concluded. "I'd like to keep playing for as far ahead as I can imagine."

That's good news for everybody but netminders on fifteen NHL teams.

PIT MARTIN After upsetting the once-mighty Boston Bruins, 1972 winners of the coveted Stanley Cup, in five games during the opening round of the 1973 playoffs, the New York Rangers looked forward to their first Cup win in thirty-three years. Rated as overwhelming underdogs upon entering the post-season classic, the Rangers displayed puck prowess the likes of which had rarely been seen in Madison Square Garden. Perhaps they had a right to be overconfident going into their semifinal series.

"We can handle those guys the same way we handled the Bruins," Brad Park, New York's All-Star defenseman, chirped when asked what he thought of the Rangers' next opponent.

"Those guys" happened to be the Chicago Black Hawks, winners of their quarter-final series against St. Louis also

in five games. Like Emile Francis of the Rangers, coach
Billy Reay of the Black Hawks had never known the satis-
faction of winning The Stanley Cup. At the Hawks' helm
since 1963, Reay twice guided his team to the final playoff
round, only to be edged by the Montreal Canadiens on
both occasions. Reay was hungry for hockey's supreme
trophy and he induced the same ravenous appetite in his
players.

The result?—while the Rangers patted themselves on the
back for their convincing decision over the Bruins, the
Black Hawks took nothing for granted and methodically
went about the task of gaining one of the two final playoff
berths.

One thing was certain—if the Hawks were to defeat
New York, they would have to generate a game plan that
would not only throttle the Rangers' explosive offense, but
exploit the weaknesses in their injury-plagued defense. A
supreme two-way effort was needed, and when it comes to
skaters proficient in play at either end of the rink, Chicago boasts one of the best in center Hubert Jacques "Pit"
Martin.

A native of Noranda, Quebec, the thirty-year-old
French-speaking center began his professional career in
1963 with the Detroit Red Wings. Unfortunately for Pit,
the Wings were well-stocked at the pivot position, and he
was shuttled back and forth between the parent club and
Detroit's Pittsburgh affiliate in the American League during the next two years. Then on 30 December 1965 Martin got the break for which he'd been waiting.

"I was home at my apartment in Pittsburgh," the
speedy skater recalled, "when the phone rang. It was Baz
Bastien [general manager of the Hornets]. 'Pit,' he said,
'you're going to Toronto and you're playing there Saturday.'

"I thought I was going to join the Red Wings in Toronto, but then Baz told me that I would be playing for
the Boston Bruins instead. It was a shock at the time but
it worked out for the best."

The deal was Martin in exchange for veteran left wing
Parker MacDonald. One enthusiastic Boston sportswriter
termed the trade "the biggest steal since the $1,219,000
Brinks' robbery." But Pit had self-doubts.

"I didn't know what to expect with the Bruins," he recalled. "I drove to Toronto and met the team at a meeting. I found it tough going from the AHL to the NHL. It took me about four or five games to get back to myself."

Once adjusted, though, the 5-8, 165-pounder left no doubts that he belonged in the big leagues. He netted 16 goals in 41 games for the Bruins during that 1965-66 season, and four of the tallies came in a single game against Pit's future team, the Black Hawks.

"Sure, I remember that night," he said, grinning. "My first shift on the ice, I got a pass from the corner right off the bat and had the whole side of the net to shoot at, but I missed by a foot. I was mad! Then I came down again with the identical chance. Only this time I didn't miss. I said to myself that I wanted to score more than one goal in this game.

"Then in the second period, I got the puck in the middle of their zone and turned around as I shot. It went into the net. In the second period, Johnny Bucyk dug the puck out of the corner and passed it to me. I let it go on my backhand and again it went in. I thought it would be impossible to score another, but in the third period I came out of a scramble in front of the net with the puck and let go with a slap shot from fifteen feet out. Again it went in, and the crowd really yelled."

Pit was even more impressive the following season, scoring 20 goals for the then-lowly Boston team. But former general manager Milt Schmidt was convinced that his player's lack of size and strength was directly responsible for the club's last-place finish. Not only was Martin small but he was also one of the few Bruins who had performed well enough to be classified as "trade bait." It was inevitable that he would be dealt away.

A deal was finally consummated with Chicago, which would prove to be one of the most one-sided exchanges in sports. The Bruins sent Martin, defenseman Gilles Marotte, and spare goaltender Jack Norris to the Windy City in return for centers Phil Esposito and Fred Stanfield and right wing Ken Hodge. Esposito, Hodge and Stanfield went on to star with the Bruins and were instrumental in lifting the team out of its perennial niche in the cellar, but little has been said or written about Martin's contribution to the Black Hawks. Since joining the team in 1967, the slick center has averaged 24 goals and 39 assists, despite missing a total of 38 games due to assorted injuries.

Statistics are only half the story for Martin, though. He has developed into one of the game's premier defensive specialists as well. Pit's performance is a study in perpetual motion—forechecking to force opponent's mistakes in the offensive zone, a hasty retreat to lend a hand back of the blueline, then up ice again with a renewed scoring threat. It's no wonder that he was one of the outstanding performers in Chicago's Stanley Cup semi-final upset victory in five games over the Rangers.

With the series standing at 2-1 in favor of Chicago, New York's Madison Square Garden was to be the site of game four. The pundits were predicting a comeback for the Rangers, who can be invincible on their home ice.

But the Black Hawks jumped out in front in the first period on a deflected 50-foot slap shot by left wing Dennis Hull. Then, Ranger captain Vic Hadfield deadlocked the score towards the end of the second stanza by lifting a backhander over Chicago goalie Tony Esposito's right shoulder.

The third period opened with both teams playing cautious hockey. Neither club was able to capture the edge in play. Midway through the session, Ranger defenseman Brad Park stickhandled in the center zone but momentarily lost control of the puck. Martin, who was diligently forechecking, snatched the disc from Park's stick and skated in alone on New York goaltender Eddie Giacomin. Rather than fake to the left or right, trying to force the goalie to commit himself, Pit bore straight in and blasted a wrist shot between Giacomin's pads and into the net. Although Hull added another goal late in the period for a final 3-1 score, Martin's marker was the decisive tally in both the game *and* the series. The Rangers never recovered their Stanley Cup drive and Chicago wrapped up the series at home by a score of 4-1. It was no surprise to Martin-watchers when Pit scored a three-goal hat-trick against Montreal in the finals, which the Black Hawks lost in six games. One wonders if Chicago is capable of a Cup win. If one Hubert Jacques Martin continues to play like he's worth $1,219,000, then coach Billy Reay's long and bitter frustration may finally be ended in 1974.

STAN MIKITA He sat in the Chicago Black Hawks dressing room early in the evening of 3 May 1973. He was not
supposed to play in The Stanley Cup match against the
Montreal Canadiens at Chicago Stadium. His thumb had
been painfully injured and it seemed impossible for him
to hold his hockey stick. At best he would sit at the end
of the bench and root his teammates to a hoped-for
victory.

But Stan Mikita is cut from a very special cloth. It
would take more than an agonizing hand injury to keep
the thirty-three-year-old Czech-born center out of the
lineup. Somehow, Stan had to find a way of easing the
pain.

"First," he remembered, "I tried a metal splint but that
didn't have the feel I wanted. I threw that away and tried
a sponge which I taped to my finger. There still was pain
and I couldn't get much whip into my shot but at least I
was able to play."

More than that, he led Chicago to a 7-4 victory over
Montreal by scoring a goal and setting up two others.
Stan's goal gave Chicago what had seemed to be an insur-
mountable 4-0 lead in the game. But late in the third
period Montreal had narrowed the count to 5-4 and
nearly tied the score in the final minute as Frank Mahovlich missed an open net while his adversary, Mikita,
looked on in temporary horror-turned-joy. "I could have
kissed Frank," laughed Mikita after the game. "I don't
know how he missed."

In the end Chicago was the team that missed winning
The Stanley Cup but through no fault of Mikita. Despite
the finger injury and the aftereffects of a broken heel suffered late in the regular season, Stan played one of the
most extraordinary seasons in his long National Hockey
League career.

With Bobby Hull gone to the World Hockey Association, Stan was expected to lead the Chicago sextet; and that he did. He scored 27 goals and 56 assists for 83 points in only 57 games, guiding Chicago to first place in the West Division and the Clarence Campbell Bowl. A season earlier he had scored only 65 points, his lowest output since his first full season in Chicago (1960-61), and the talk was that he was washed-up. Nobody knew about the criticism more than Stan himself.

"I heard and read all the stuff about my being finished," he said, "and it hurt my pride. I realized that the previous couple of seasons had not been my best but they weren't all that bad either. We broke in a few new guys on my line in the past couple of seasons and, besides that, I hadn't been 100 per cent physically."

Many critics believe two factors helped change Mikita for the better—intense training with Team Canada in August 1972 which prepared him in advance for the season; and Bobby Hull's departure to Winnipeg.

"The best thing that ever happened to Stan," said a member of the Los Angeles Kings who knows Mikita well, "was Bobby getting out of town. All of a sudden Stan became number one man on the team after being number two for too long. It was a terrific boost for his ego and he made the most of it."

The question about Hull's absence was put to Mikita and he allowed that it might have had a positive effect on him. "I worked harder last season," Stan admitted. "We missed Bobby. There was no way that we could lose a guy like him and not feel it. When Bobby was here everybody looked to him as a leader. After he left I sort of nominated myself as our leader. There was a lot of pressure on us to win without Bobby, and since I had been around for a long time I hoped that I could get a little respect from the players and that they would follow me. But I also expected everybody else to be a leader in his own way. People waited for us to collapse but we didn't. We had too many good players for that to happen."

Stan himself did collapse, through no fault of his own, during a game against the Atlanta Flames which resulted in his heel injury and the fear that he would miss the homestretch of the 1972-73 season and, even worse, the playoffs.

"I was flat on my butt," Mikita recalled, "heading for the boards, and I stuck my foot out to try and cushion the blow. I guess I made a messy job of it. God, the pain. I don't think I ever felt so much before, all at one time."

The accident was diagnosed as a spiral fracture of the oscalcis bone. Translated, it meant that whenever he stopped on his heel—which was always when he skated—it meant more pain. But by playoff time he was almost cured, as proven by his sterling efforts against the St. Louis Blues, followed by the amazing five-game upset of the New York Rangers in the semi-finals.

"I'm skating better than I was before," Stan went on. "Not as much wasted motion, going to certain points instead of all over the ice. I'm just letting the legs fall into place. Not as much effort and more confidence."

Just about the only time Mikita betrayed any lack of confidence was in December 1972. The Black Hawks were attempting to leave Chicago for a game in Toronto but learned that no planes would be departing from O'Hare Airport in The Windy City. Instead, they headed for Midway Airport on the chance that they might get a flight there.

"Somewhere along the way," reported *Toronto Daily Star* columnist Milt Dunnell, "Mikita disappeared. Somehow, he had missed the connection."

Stan finally made it to Toronto and then explained his temporary absence. "It wasn't an accident," he said. "The uncertainty and change of plans just got to me. There had been two major crashes in Chicago during the weeks preceding that and I knew I was going to be uncomfortable all the time we were in the air. I just wasn't willing to take it. So, I took the morning plane and got in without any trouble."

The only other trouble in Mikita's life recently has been a chronic back problem. "I'd hate to think how many times I've thought about hanging it up for good," he said. "But a few summers ago I phoned my plumber for a job around the house and he gave me the name of a doctor. I went to him and it's been good ever since."

Good for Stan, bad for enemy goaltenders. Montreal's

Ken Dryden will second that. He'll not soon forget that night of 8 May 1973 when the Black Hawks fired eight goals behind him to defeat the Canadiens, 8-7. Mikita led the scoring parade with two goals and two assists. Chicago was down, three games to one, before that contest at The Forum, and earned themselves a one-game reprieve with the upset victory, which surprised Stan as much as anyone.

"I've never seen a game like it before," he said, "much less played in one. We got all those goals because we had to open up the game and take chances. We had to do anything we could to win. We couldn't afford to play a defensive game. But I never expected to see fifteen pucks go into the net."

Montreal whipped Chicago the next time out but nobody blamed the Hawks. In the final minute of the match 20,000 fans rose as one and delivered a standing ovation to their gallant heroes. You can be sure that a healthy portion of that applause was directed at the most gallant of them all, Stan Mikita.

BOBBY ORR By any set of reasonable hockey standards the 1972-73 season was not a good one for Bobby Orr, the all-everything for Boston's Bruins. He was forced to miss the Team Canada-Russia series in September 1972 because his operated-upon knee was slow to heal; he failed to start the season on defense for the same reason and his Bruins lost their defense of first place and The Stanley Cup.

Bobby himself was unhappy with the final results of the campaign. Yet, when the tabulation was completed in voting for The Norris Trophy, Orr had won it for the sixth consecutive season, and was reaffirmed as the best defenseman in the National Hockey League, if not the best all-around player in the world.

In some respects it was an amazing development because rumors had surfaced during the year that Orr's knee was so fragile he might never play hockey again. However, an incident in November 1972 against the New York Islanders convinced skeptics that Orr was still capable of a comeback.

It was Bobby's first NHL game since his absence. Midway in the game he launched one of his headlong rushes along the right boards but was sized up and bodychecked perfectly by defenseman Jim Mair. Orr hit the ice with a thud and, for a split-second, the season hung in the balance for him. But Bobby recovered, clambered to his skates and led the Bruins to a 7-3 victory. "The most important thing," said Bruins boss Harry Sinden, "was that he landed on the knee after a hard check and then tumbled to the ice, but recovered without serious aftereffects."

"Bobby is something" said former Bruins goalie Ed Johnston, "isn't he?"

He is all things to all people, and not all that complimentary either. But as a hockey player, Orr is all star. Bobby himself may not admit that he commands the Bruins ship and that when he decides to take charge the game tilts in Boston's favor, but others know this to be true.

"Orr is so great," said teammate Derek Sanderson, "because he doesn't consciously try to take charge; he just does it, automatically."

"Even when he's not moving well," said Rangers captain Vic Hadfield, "Orr still controls the play."

During the regular 1972-73 season he scored 29 goals and 72 assists for 101 points, third only to Phil Esposito, and Bobby missed 15 games. But respected critics don't consider the two in the same class; Orr is alone, well ahead of Esposito. He is the only Boston athlete who can be compared with Ted Williams.

"If a hockey player could bat .400," wrote columnist Harold Kaese of the *Boston Globe*, "Bobby Orr would be the man. He is a master of his craft, a virtuoso. Ted Williams, the brash one, was a more exciting sports personality than Bobby Orr, the shy one, but in their professions they are comparable performers."

"In my 37 years in the NHL," said ex-Bruins manager Milt Schmidt, "Bobby is the greatest player I have ever

seen in the past, the greatest player at present, and if anyone greater should show up, I just hope the Good Lord
has me around here to see him.

Orr not only has taken on Messianic qualities for the
Bruins, but for the NHL as well. In an era when big-
league hockey is spreading its wings to new areas of North
America, Orr remains the most saleable commodity the
shinny moguls have to offer. And nobody knows it better
than Orr's attorney Al Eagleson of Toronto.

"Bobby is the only player who can help out the low-
drawing teams in the NHL," said Eagleson. "For example,
in Oakland, Orr once played there on a Sunday night and
drew 10,500. St. Louis came there on a Wednesday and
drew 3,000. In Los Angeles, Orr drew 12,700, the next
night against St. Louis the crowd was only 7,200. Vancouver's manager says he could sell an extra 30,000-40,000
tickets when Orr is in town."

Orr's deportment on ice cannot be questioned in terms
of his abilities. When he entered the NHL at age eighteen
he displayed the strong skating, mighty shot, unwavering
courage, and keen instincts that comprise the superstar.
What's more, he played a vital role in changing hockey
from a bush-league low-paying sport into one of the
higher-salaried team games.

Until Bobby Orr came along, nobody but nobody in
professional hockey—and that includes the super-dupers
like Gordie Howe and Bobby Hull—earned more than
$40,000.

Orr, with help from Eagleson, changed that. Bobby now
is collecting $1,000,000 spread over five years and has
helped lift the salaries of his colleagues in the process.
Friends and foes alike toast Orr like no other athlete in
their profession.

"He is," said Bobby Hull, "the greatest young hockey
player that's come along since I've been here and that's 17
years. He controls the puck. If he doesn't have the room
to skate with it he'll give it to a teammate and then bust
to get it back. Most guys, after they've given it up, will
just watch it go. Bobby takes off and when he hits your
blue line he's streaking."

Dave Keon of Toronto added: "Orr's success comes
down to his mastery of the basics. He's so quick. He antic-

ipates extremely well. He wants to be good and he has great natural ability. The combination is hard to beat."

To many young fans, Orr is more than just a hockey player. He is a sensitive human being who will take time out to discuss his favorite sport with youngsters such as Frank Fitzgerald, a ten-year-old from Preston, Ontario.

Following a game at Maple Leaf Gardens in Toronto last season, Bobby listened with rapt attention as Frank, who is gradually going blind, told Orr how the kids play hockey at the Ontario School for the Blind in Brampton, Ontario. The lads use a tin can instead of a puck and chase around the ice by listening to the rattle.

Youths like Frank Fitzgerald worship Bobby Orr's every move which explains why there was so much concern across Canada and the United States when Bobby had so much trouble recuperating from his knee surgery. His failure to be in the Team Canada lineup and photos of an obviously overweight Orr in the fall of 1972 sent reverberations of fear all the way to Boston Garden.

"Yeah," Orr admitted, "I was up as high as 214 pounds. My normal playing weight is about 185. How did I let myself balloon up? I couldn't do anything at all. No tennis, nothing, and I just ate myself up to that weight. I love to eat. I still do. But with exercise it stays under control."

By January 1973 Orr was getting all that exercise—on the ice. His return to the Bruins lineup converted them from also-rans to contenders. In February, when the New York Rangers thought they had second place locked up, Orr piloted the Bruins to a heady winning streak that ultimately landed Boston in second ahead of New York.

Bobby's effort didn't surprise everybody. There were many who sensed that once he put on the blades he would be the miracle man of yore. "People were saying that he couldn't come back after three knee operations," said Montreal Canadiens coach Scotty Bowman, "but I never doubted it. He was able to do it with no trouble at all because he's a super athlete. Nobody dominates a game like he does; and hockey's a difficult game to dominate. When Orr is on the ice the game changes completely. You tend to hold back for fear he'll break out of a one-on-one situation."

Stopping Orr has been a puzzle to NHL coaches ever

since Bobby entered the league. Some critics believe the Rangers solved the puzzle last spring when they eliminated Boston in five games from the first Stanley Cup round.

"We watched films of Orr in action," said Rangers goalie Ed Giacomin. "After studying the films we decided that the best way to keep him from hurting us was to flood his side. We kept throwing the puck in and making him go back and chase it. You do that to anyone and he's going to get tired. Eventually, it hurt his game."

Bobby scored once in 20 shots. When necessary, he was double-teamed; and when the fifth game was over, Orr was a very dejected hockey player.

But should the opposition be comforted by the results of April 1973, they had better be careful. Take it from Johnny McLellan, the former Toronto Maple Leafs coach. "They thought Orr was finished at the start of 1972-73," said McLellan, "but when he came back it looked like he'd never been away. It's always a mistake to count him out!"

BRAD PARK New York Rangers defenseman Brad Park became so identified as the National Hockey League's *second-best* defenseman—behind Boston's Bobby Orr— that the Avis Rent-A-Car Company hired him to do their "We're Number Two" commercials. Like Avis, Park hopes, someday, to be number one.

A lot of people, Park included, thought this would happen during the 1972-73 season. It was to be the Rangers' year, mostly because they, unlike the Bruins and Chicago Black Hawks, were unharmed by World Hockey Association raids. Park had received a contract estimated at $200,000 a year for five years and was expected to play the best hockey of his life.

He did average better than a point a game, accumulating 53 points (10 goals and 43 assists), but he played in only 52 out of the Rangers' 78 regular season contests; and that, as much as anything, helps explain why the New Yorkers finished in third rather than first place.

Like Orr, Park is the key to both his team's offense *and* defense. His defensive talents are obvious. He employs a "submarine" bodycheck better than any contemporary defenseman, and is a marvel at sending the puck out of the New York danger zone to freedom.

"Brad," said Rangers right wing Rod Gilbert, "moves the puck up so we don't have to work like devils in our own end. That leaves us free to concentrate on offense at the other end. He always thinks far ahead of the play and that results in more scoring opportunities for the forwards. When he gets hurt, we go into a slump."

Brad realizes that he is a defenseman first and defensemen are supposed to hit, a fact he learned years ago. "My philosophy," said Park, "is that an opponent isn't likely to score many goals from a horizontal position. Whenever possible, I try to throw a good, legal bodycheck. Whenever we do that, one of the Rangers' statisticians records it as a 'hit.' In my first few years in the league I averaged seven to eight 'hits' per game."

Long before the game actually begins, Park begins thinking about his enemy and precisely which opponent might be hittable. His coach, Emile Francis, often posts the lineups in the dressing room, enabling Park to concentrate on his foe.

"You sit there waiting," Brad continued, "and the waiting becomes such a process that you can't wait for that first 'hit' to get you moving on the ice, and you hope that it comes early. Thinking positively, as the aggressor, I'm likely to deliver that hit rather than get it. It's a lot better that way, because the *hittee* can get hurt."

But Park didn't deliver enough hits in time last season. Once, Ed Van Impe of the Philadelphia Flyers nailed him on the follow-through of a slapshot, and Brad landed on a hospital bed. His absence disrupted the Rangers' momentum, and upon his return there were recurring rumors that Brad was still not right. The confrontation between the Rangers and Bruins in the first round of the 1973 Stanley Cup playoffs would be a good test.

The 6-0, 190-pound Park had been gunning for the Boston challenge for a full year. In the 1972 Boston-New York final, the Bruins won The Cup in six games and Orr outplayed Park. Brad eyed the 1973 round with unusual severity. "During the season," he said, "a player can afford to make a mistake. During the playoffs, you can't. You win and make more money or you go home."

Rarely have New Yorkers enjoyed a more satisfying playoff than in April 1973. The Rangers wiped out Boston in five games and dreams of Stanley Cup champagne danced in Brad's head. "After we beat Boston," he recalled, "I felt we were going to win it all. We came home for a rest and then went out to Chicago to open the series. We beat them in the first game at Chicago Stadium and I was sure we had the series in the bag."

So did most New Yorkers. But the Black Hawks had different ideas. They rallied in the second game to win in The Windy City and tie the series at one apiece. Then, in a startling reversal, the Black Hawks won the next three games to deflate Brad and his mates.

"We played well enough," said Park, "but the puck bounced wrong and the breaks were bad, but I sure as hell couldn't see it that way after the final game of the series in Chicago. I remember when it ended I looked across the dressing room at Emile Francis and I thought he had done such a great job for all of us and I felt that we had let him down. I felt awful."

For Brad, it was his fifth consecutive try for The Stanley Cup and his fifth failure. He seemed to take it harder than ever, because 1972-73 was supposed to be *the* year. "It's a long, long cycle," Park explained. "You start with the hopes in training camp; the back-busting at the start of the season when you want to get off to a fast start, then the jockeying for positions down the stretch for The Cup series, and then the series itself and the knowledge that you have to win not one but three different rounds for it to mean anything."

In a sense Park was lucky. His early training enabled him to accept defeat without thinking it was the end of the world. Winning, of course, was important; but playing to the best of his ability was regarded as the single most significant aspect of Brad's early training. If that was accomplished all other good things would fall into place.

The development of Brad from peewee to professional is a case study in how parents *can* help their children. Park's father, Bob, and his mother, Betty, prudently but diligently advised their son once they realized he had special skating and stickhandling gifts.

"Brad started playing hockey when he was five," Mrs. Park recalled. "He couldn't see why he couldn't play if his older brother, who was three years older, already was in the game. Brad bugged his dad until finally they let him play goal. When they found out he could skate they put him up front."

Young hockey players often hone their skills to sharpness at the cost of destroying a house. In the Park home there were constant seismic reverberations as Brad bounced pucks off shingles, steps, and garage doors.

"By the time we moved to another home," said Mrs. Park, "there were more dents in the wood panelling than there were nails."

Both Bob and Betty Park kept their lines out to Brad as he moved up the hockey ladder. It was not unusual for Bob to be on the phone to Brad after an NHL game in his rookie year, always seeking to improve the boy. And Betty would get her lessons in, too.

"I'm very critical of him," she admitted. "If he doesn't hit within the first few minutes on the ice I don't think he's going to play the kind of game he's capable of playing. We always have felt that constructive criticism is helpful. Brad always needs an incentive." Needless to say, Bobby Orr has provided some of the best incentive available for Brad. A Toronto columnist remarked that had Orr arrived in another era, the praise for Park would even be more lavish.

Right now, Park is, as his Avis commercial indicates, "number two." He has to be until he finishes on top and plays for a Stanley Cup-winner the way Orr has. The way Brad tells it, that will be accomplished by the middle of May 1974.

"It's going to be different during the 1973-74 season," Park predicted. "This time I won't watch The Stanley Cup finals on television. In May 1974 somebody else will be watching me!"

GIL PERREAULT Late last season George "Punch" Imlach, the man who built the Buffalo Sabres into a playoff contender within three seasons, delivered one of his typically unequivocal statements. "That kid," said Imlach pointing at curly-haired Gil Perreault, "is the best center in the game—bar none. There's no way anyone can get Perreault out of Buffalo."

Punch had good reason for his pro-Perreault propaganda. Playing all of his team's 78 regular season games, the 5-11, 183-pound French-Canadian led the Sabres in scoring with 28 goals and 60 assists for 88 points.

But it wasn't so much how many points Perreault accumulated but rather how he fashioned them. More often than not, a Perreault goal or one of Gil's assists was a work of art. The fans who jammed Montreal's Forum on 10 April 1973 will attest to that.

Buffalo and Montreal were locked in 2-2 playoff tie and now were skating in sudden death overtime when Sabres' coach Joe Crozier called Perreault over to the bench and barked at him. "Enough is enough. Go through that whole bloody team and score a goal!"

Gil skated back to the face-off circle and crouched opposite his adversary, Jacques Lemaire. The puck was dropped and Perreault took it from Lemaire as easy as taking candy from a baby.

Gil then jiggled the puck on the end of his stick, searching for a free member of his "French Connection" line, either René Robert or Rick Martin. He noticed that Robert had slipped past Canadiens defenseman Jacques Laperriere. "I saw René right away," said Perreault, "and didn't even have to look up to lay a pass to him."

Teammates say that Gil's passes are as soft as cotton candy and just as delicious. This one was a 40-foot piece of perfection, enabling Robert to skate in unmolested on goalie Ken Dryden for the winning score. The goal went to Robert but the next day the headlines rightfully belonged to Gil. *The Montreal Gazette* ran an eight column banner, "PERREAULT PULLS OUT A WILD ONE," which enabled Imlach to walk the streets of Montreal with a three-inch grin.

Punch obviously is biased in favor of Perreault since Gil was his number one draft choice in June 1970, but other more objective hockey people have jumped on Gil's bandwagon in the past year. "Perreault," said Boston's superstar Bobby Orr, "is easily the most exciting player I've seen come into the league."

What is it that makes Gil so exciting? For one thing he is a splendid skater and for another he can pass the puck as well as he shoots it, which is hard and accurately or soft and accurately, depending on the occasion. He more than anybody was responsible for Buffalo's finishing in fourth place in the NHL's East Division ahead of the Detroit Red Wings.

One of the Sabres' most important wins was accomplished last February at Buffalo's tumultuous Auditorium when Gil scored the decisive goal against the New York Rangers. Apart from moving Buffalo over Detroit in the playoff race it marked the Sabres' fifth win over the Rangers in six games.

"To get his winning goal against New York," wrote Mark Mulvoy of *Sports Illustrated,* "Perreault, his bowed legs working with deceptive speed and perfect balance, gave defenseman Dale Rolfe a hip fake, two leg fakes, a couple of shoulder fakes, a hatful of head fakes and a few eye blinks, all the while controlling the puck with deft moves of the stick. As Rolfe reeled, Perreault fired the puck past goaltender Ed Giacomin."

Perreault has reached the pinnacle so fast that respected critics already are comparing him with the supreme skater of Boston, Bobby Orr. "They're different," said former Buffalo center Don Marshall. "Orr is more of a give-and-go player. He'll get the play started by giving a pass. Gil beats the man himself. He does it all. He gives you a quick look at the puck and gets it back close to his body very quickly. If you make a move for the puck, you're caught flat-footed as he goes by you. If you do get a piece

Chicago Black Hawks center
STAN MIKITA (r) finds an
opening in the Islanders' defense—and goalie pads.
Photo By Harvey Cohen

BERNIE PARENT staggers
back with the impact of a
shot in a March 1973 game
he played with the now-de-
funct Philadelphia Blazers.
PARENT is currently with his
original expansion team, the
NHL Flyers.

Photo By Harvey Cohen

New England Whalers goalie AL SMITH goes to his knees to prevent a score, as defenseman BRAD SELWOOD looks on for the rebound.
Photo By Harvey Cohen

CRAIG REICHMUTH of the New York Golden Blades (formerly the Raiders), eyes the puck just released by former Philadelphia Blazers goalie BERNIE PARENT, now starring for the Philly Flyers.
Photo By Harvey Cohen

Ageless Montreal Canadiens captain HENRI RICHARD awaits the drop of the puck for a face-off.
Photo By Harvey Cohen

Well-traveled (five NHL teams, before becoming manager of the Quebec Nordiques) goalie JACQUES PLANTE pauses for a post-game interview during April 1973 as a Bruin.
Photo By Terry Foley

Speedy New York Golden Blades center BOBBY SHEE-HAN has clear sailing for a rush up ice.
Photo By Harvey Cohen

Pittsburgh's SYL APPS (R) has his stick down for the face-off. Islander winger BILLY HARRIS anticipates the result.
Photo By Michael Trott

Pittsburgh Penguins star GREG POLIS (22) shoots at Islanders' goalie BILLY SMITH through a crowd. Defensemen NEIL NICHOLSON (helmet), and GERRY HART try to block the shot, as POLIS' teammate ROBIN BURNS hopes for a tip-in.
Photo By Michael Trott

STAN MIKITA of the Black Hawks tries to elude Ranger defenseman RON HARRIS in pursuit of the puck.
Photo By Roberto Borea

RON WARD's WHA record-setting fifth goal gets a good push into the net, as helpless Ottawa goalie GILLES GRATTON looks on. (The Ottawa Nationals are now the Toronto Toros). WARD was later traded to the Vancouver Blazers.
Photo By Harvey Cohen

Classy All-Star defense-
man GUY LAPOINTE
starts a Montreal rush
from behind his net.
Photo By Harvey Cohen

Promising young Cal-
ifornia Golden Seals
goaltender GILLES
MELOCHE readies him-
self for an onslaught
of rubber.
Photo By Harvey Cohen

Ranger defenseman
BRAD PARK winds up
for a slap shot in a
game against the St.
Louis Blues.
Photo By Roberto Borea

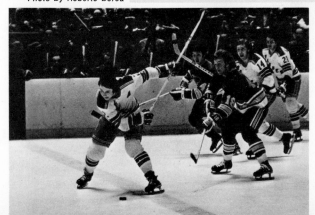

HARRIS meets HARRIS, as Minnesota's defenseman TED (L) matches up with Islanders' winger BILLY, who is no relation.

Photo By Harvey Cohen

Slick Rangers center JEAN RATELLE stickhandles away from Boston Bruin DEREK SANDERSON (27), as RATELLE's linemate VIC HADFIELD yells encouragement.

Photo By Roberto Borea

Dynamic Chicago Black Hawk winger DENNIS HULL, no longer in the shadow of his older brother BOBBY, pauses during a stoppage in play.

Photo By Roberto Borea

Bruin super-defenseman BOBBY ORR has the puck, as usual.

Photo By Roberto Borea

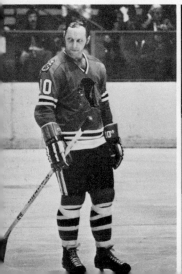

All-Star left wing FRANK MA-
HOVLICH of the Canadiens
watches a play develop.
Photo By Roberto Borea

Winnipeg Jets' BOBBY HULL
lets loose with one of his
patented slapshots.
Photo By Melchior Di Giacomo

The old guard meets the new,
as veteran HENRI RICHARD
(background) confronts Ranger center WALT TKACZUK.
Photo By Terry Foley

Bruins star BOBBY ORR goes
all out in an effort to make a
poke check. *Photo By Roberto Borea*

Chicago Black Hawks All-Star netminder TONY ESPOSITO eyes a deflected shot as it flies into the corner.
Photo By Roberto Borea

Defenseman BRAD PARK of the Rangers (1) is outnumbered by the Bruins' DON MARCOTTE (21) and BOBBY ORR.
Photo By Roberto Borea

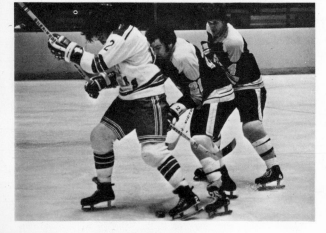

Boston Superman BOBBY ORR watches the puck as teammates KEN HODGE (8) and WAYNE CASHMAN close in on Ranger ROD GILBERT.
Photo By Roberto Borea

of him, you find he's very strong. He can overpower you."

Orr put it another way: "Gil is always tempting you to go for the puck. His head and shoulders go one way, his legs go the other way and the puck is doing something else. When I first saw it, I couldn't believe it."

Which is precisely what onlookers were saying about Perreault ever since he began playing organized hockey in the province of Quebec.

Gil was the talk of Canadian junior hockey for several years. In the 1969-70 season he scored 51 goals during the regular campaign and then added 34 in 28 playoff games. He became, in a teen-aged sort of way, what Maurice "Rocket" Richard had been to the Montreal Canadiens during the Forties and Fifties. When handsome Gil would gather the puck for the Junior Canadiens, people in The Forum would chant, *"On veut Perreault!"* (We want Perreault!)

In pre-expansion hockey days a French-speaking player such as Perreault enjoyed an almost 90 per cent chance of landing on the Canadien's roster. But that was long ago. The normally medieval-thinking NHL owners finally realized that expansion teams need good young talent and Imlach decided to hang on to Perreault, although the temptation to deal him to Sammy Pollock, manager of the Canadiens, was immense. However, in a weak moment, Imlach allowed he would make a deal.

"All Sam's gotta do," said Imlach, "is gimme Jean Beliveau, Jacques Lemaire, Henri Richard, Jacques Laperriere, J.C. Tremblay and a few more of them."

Which explains why Gilbert Perreault checked into the Buffalo Sabres' training base one afternoon in September 1970. Once he shook himself loose of the press clippings it became apparent that this was a superb hockey player.

"He looked like a million dollars on skates," said Red Burnett, the veteran hockey analyst for *The Toronto Daily Star.*

It would be easy to say that the pressure was on Perreault from the moment he skated out on the ice for Buffalo in a regular NHL game; but that's nonsense. Perreault, as so many young NHL players are realizing these days, knew that no matter what happened he was in the big-leagues to stay—at least for this season. He knew that

his three-year $25,000-a-year contract meant that he was
"in like Flynn" and that the talent-starved Sabres needed
him more than he needed Buffalo.

Perreault came along with the usual publicity harangue.
Somebody remembered that Gil's first organized team was
in Victoriaville, Quebec, the very same town where a chap
named Jean Beliveau learned his hockey. And then word
got around that Perreault had patterned himself after Beliveau. Like Beliveau, Perreault would rather play hockey
than fight, they said.

"Perreault," Mulvoy agreed, "most nearly deserves close
comparison with the majestic Beliveau, because only he
skates with such stately grace and sang-froid."

Unlike Beliveau, Perreault won the Calder Trophy as
NHL rookie of the year. In Gil's second season his point
total was 74, a gain of two over his freshman campaign.
A year later he had jumped his total by 14 points.

"I'm not sure hockey fans realize how good Gil really
is," said teammate Tracy Pratt. "To me, he's already the
best center iceman in the league and it's only his fourth
season as a pro."

Who knows, four years from now they may be saying
he's better than Beliveau.

JEAN RATELLE In the icy jungle that is the National
Hockey League the guiding rule, as set forth by Toronto
Maple Leafs founder Conn Smythe, has been: *If you
can't beat 'em in the alley, you can't beat 'em on the ice!*

A cantankerous manager, Smythe once announced that
he would fire any player on his club who won the NHL's
Lady Byng Trophy, awarded to the stickhandler "adjudged
to have exhibited the best type of sportsmanship and
gentlemanly conduct combined with a high standard of
playing ability."

The theory has been that any "goody two-shoes" who

wins the Lady Byng has no more place in the blood-and-guts atmosphere of a big-league hockey rink than a snowball has in a desert.

Enter long, lean Joseph Gilbert Jean Ratelle to put that theory to rest once and for all.

At thirty-three years of age, the 6-1, 175-pound French-Canadian center from Lac St. Jean, Quebec, is, perhaps, the best *and* cleanest scorer ever to skate on a sheet of ice. Ratelle is *so* much the nice guy that the NHL has run out of awards for him.

In addition to the Lady Byng, he also has won the Bill Masterton Trophy as "the player who best exemplifies the qualities of perseverance, sportsmanship, and dedication to hockey."

Why, then, haven't the NHL carnivores devoured Ratelle by now?

"Simple," says hard-guy Boston Bruin Derek Sanderson, a pro player who admittedly wouldn't hesitate to break his sister's leg if she played on the other team. "Jean commands so much respect because of his ability and his style, it's impossible to get yourself mad enough at him to try any dirty stuff."

Ranger defenseman Brad Park, who has been known to adapt the jungle code to the ice, calls his linemate, Ratelle, "our straight arrow." Park explains: "Ratty is without a doubt the model hockey player, totally dedicated to the sport and the team. He plays hockey according to the rule book and would never even *think* of elbowing or smashing a guy or doing anything physical. He's just a beautiful player."

Ratelle's system demonstrates that if nice guys don't quite finish first, they do finish pretty close to the top. Despite a broken ankle that hospitalized him for fifteen games two seasons ago, Ratelle landed third in the scoring race—right behind league leaders Phil Esposito and Bobby Orr, of The Stanley-Cup-champion Boston Bruins.

To knowledgeable critics of the game who prefer form to statistics, Ratelle's graceful skating style and pinpoint passing lifted him to a plateau above even Orr and Esposito. "If Jean hadn't been injured two seasons ago," says Phil Goyette, a former center who has played for champion teams in Montreal and St. Louis as well as for the

Rangers, "he would have beaten out Bobby Orr for the Hart [most valuable player] Trophy."

Ratelle has made a habit of bringing capacity crowds (17,250) to their feet at Madison Square Garden. Typical was the night when Jean dipsy-doodled through the Detroit Red Wing defense like a pinball zigzagging down its course, to become the first Ranger ever to score 100 points in a season.

Minutes after the game a growing circle of newsmen crowded around the reluctant superstar in the steamy, liniment-smelling Ranger dressing room. Teammate Ted Irvine stood motionless at the edge of the crowd, impressed as a schoolboy by Ratelle's dignified manner as Jean fielded questions.

Finally, Irvine turned to a friend. "I'll tell you something," the rugged Ranger forward volunteered. "If I'm ever on the bench and see any guy take a cheap shot at Ratty, I swear I'll come right over the boards and go after the guy, even if it costs me a fine for doing it."

Ratelle's value to the Rangers is equal to that of the left rear wheel on an automobile. Take it away and the car goes nowhere.

One team that remembers Ratelle's blitzes more vividly than others is the Vancouver Canucks. On the night of 15 February 1972 Ratelle explored completely new and different methods of scoring a three-goal hat-trick.

The 15,570 fans at the Pacific Coliseum in Vancouver had hardly settled into their theater-type seats when Jean began his act. Within 13 seconds of the opening face-off, Ratelle swooped down on the Canucks' cage like a falcon after his prey, and smacked a loose puck over goalie Dunc Wilson. Six seconds before the end of the second period a crisp pass landed on Jean's stick and faster than he could say, *"Eh, voila!"* it was in the net. These, however, were commonplace, ho-hum goals compared with what was to come.

In the final minutes of the match, Ranger defensemen Dale Rolfe and Gary Doak both received penalties, leaving New York two men short. At this point Vancouver coach Hal Laycoe removed his goaltender and added still another skater, giving the Canucks a six-skater to three-skater advantage over the Rangers.

Ranger general manager-coach Emile Francis sent in Ratelle. The orders—"Win that face-off; keep the puck from the Canucks!"

Jean slowly moved toward the red bull's-eye on the milky-white ice, eye-to-eye with Andre Boudrias of Vancouver. "All I wanted to do," says Ratelle in his French-salted English accent, "was clear the puck out of our end of the rink. I wasn't even thinking of scoring."

The linesman moved between the two crouched foes and released the six-ounce vulcanized rubber puck. It bounced on the hard ice like a frozen doughnut and ricocheted off Boudrias' skate so fast that the Canuck center momentarily lost sight of it.

"I still don't believe it," Jean recalls, describing the most spectacular goal of his 13-year professional career. "I got the puck away from Boudrias before he knew where it was. Then, all of a sudden, I noticed how wide their defense was playing, so I moved around Boudrias and just let the puck go up the middle. It went up—and up—and up—and in!"

A hockey rink is 200 feet long. When he shot the puck, Ratelle was precisely 150 feet away from the empty, yawning Vancouver goal. Since the NHL does not keep records on length of shots, there is no indication whether a longer goal was ever scored.

"I've been around hockey for a long time," says Emile Francis, who broke in as a pro in 1942, "but I don't remember ever seeing a shot scored from that far out."

It wasn't merely the length of the drive that astonished onlookers but also Ratelle's professional calm as he made the goal. "We're playing six men to their three," says Laycoe, "and he takes the puck, measures the shot, and puts it in. Unbelievable! He could try that shot again in practice and I'll bet he wouldn't hit it more than once in ten."

"It was," says Rangers' golf-oriented center, Peter Stemkowski, "like getting a two on a par-five hole."

In his next game Ratelle broke the Ranger team record of 40 goals (held by Andy Bathgate) by deflecting defenseman Jim Neilson's slapshot into the net in a game at Oakland. "I'd have to call that a lucky goal," says Jean modestly. "Jimmy's shot was on the ice and the puck just hit my stick and went into the left corner."

Ratelle's modesty can be startling at times. It's also deceptive. Those who know Ratelle insist that he is a lot more confident about his abilities than he lets on to the media.

"He's an extremely polite athlete," says Marty Blackman, a Manhattan sports representative who worked with Ratelle during a contract dispute with the Rangers' front office. "His mild manner gives people the wrong impression of Jean's tough inner fiber. When it came down to negotiating with Emile Francis, Jean was hard as nails. He knew what he wanted—what he was worth—and he didn't settle for a penny less."

Ratelle eventually signed and has more than repaid the Madison Square Garden Corporation, which owns the Rangers. Even a hard-liner like Francis admits that. "I've been coaching Ratelle for fourteen years now, starting in junior hockey," says Francis, "and I can't remember his ever having had a bad practice, let alone a bad game. He's the most consistent player I've ever seen."

All of which is rather astonishing, considering Ratelle's modest beginning as a hockey player in a tiny French-speaking hamlet some 300 miles north of Montreal.

"I started skating when I was five," Jean remembers. "I wore my father's big skates—size ten—over my socks, my shoes, and my galoshes, all together, so they'd fit. We'd go out on the frozen lake every day and just play for hours and hours."

Jean was ten years old when his family moved south to the bustling metropolis that is Montreal. Awed by his surroundings, he finally became accustomed to big-city life after being enrolled at Roussin Academy, a French-speaking Catholic school. It was there that he met his linemate-to-be, Rodrigue "Rod" Gilbert, a handsome, chunky right wing.

With Ratelle at center and Gilbert on right wing, Roussin rarely lost a hockey game until Jean suffered a broken bone in his hand at the age of fifteen. Then Gilbert left for Guelph, Ontario, to play junior hockey in the New York Rangers' farm system. Day after day, he pestered his coach with praise of his school buddy who was an even better hockey player, and Ratelle soon was invited to Guelph.

As always, hockey came easy to Jean but he encountered a major problem in another area. He discovered that *nobody* in Guelph spoke French. "It was a completely new situation for me," he recalls, "and a difficult one. Our coach, Eddie Bush, made a point of rooming the French-speaking players like me and Rod with the English players so we'd learn to speak their language."

Jean's best English teacher was an attractive sixteen-year-old who was to become his wife.

At Guelph he also learned more about being a good hockey player. He advanced up the professional ladder to Three Rivers, Quebec; Kitchener-Waterloo, Ontario; Baltimore; and, finally, New York. In the 1965-66 season he arrived in the majors to stay.

Just when it appeared that Ratelle had reached stardom in the 1966-67 season he received news that struck like a thunderbolt. Doctors suspected that his back was broken. They ordered X rays and then a delicate and complicated operation that could have ended his career at the age of twenty-six. But he recovered completely and a season later enjoyed the finest scoring record of his career. One very good reason for that was the fact that Francis put Ratelle on a line with the power-shooting Rod Gilbert and the robust Vic Hadfield. They have been together ever since.

"We're like perfectly meshed gears," says Ratelle. "We have a pretty good idea where each guy is going to be on any given play."

The sameness ends with their life-styles. Gilbert is the club's swinging bachelor and Hadfield is the team wit, using Jean Ratelle's profile as the source of much locker-room humor. "Just think, Jean," Hadfield said one day last season, "if your nose keeps on growing across your face that way, eventually it'll be in your ear!"

Ratelle shrugs off the barbs as casually as he brushes away enemy bodychecks. He is a man who knows that he is the best and he has the votes of 17,250 Madison Square Garden rooters every time he skates out on the Manhattan ice.

One night two seasons ago those fans thundered a forty-five-second standing ovation for Ratelle after he had stuffed a short hard shot under Detroit Red Wing goaltender Andy Brown. It was Jean's 102nd point in a glorious season in which he scored 109 points, highest ever on the Rangers.

As the decibel count climbed around the Rangers' bench, Hadfield skated over to Ratelle and presented him with the puck as a souvenir. An hour later, as the media hordes surrounded him with toothpick microphones and ballpoint pens, Jean said with some embarrassment, "Maybe my wife will put the puck on a plaque with the other pucks. Then we'll put the plaque in the basement where nobody can see it."

It will hang next to the Lady Byng Trophy and the Bill Masterton Trophy and the other marks of honor for the beauty of clean play in hockey—despite the people such as Conn Smythe who liken the sport to alley-fighting on ice. *New York Post* columnist Larry Merchant put it best.

"Jean Ratelle," said Merchant, "is the kind of hockey player all the ruffians would be if they had his ability."

MICKEY REDMOND When Mickey Redmond was a youngster growing up in Kirkland Lake, Ontario, he and brother Dick would disdain the usual childhood pastimes to sharpen their puck-shooting skills in the compact "Redmond Arena"—otherwise known as the basement in Mickey's house.

"Dick and I used to shoot by the hour in the cellar—when we weren't on the ice somewhere," the Red Wings' star right wing and older brother of Chicago Black Hawks defenseman Dick, reminisced recently.

"Sometimes we'd rig something in the shape of a goal, but most of the time we'd shoot at targets—usually sealers our mother would give us. I guess she cleaned up a few tons of broken glass.

"What I remember best was laying a cardboard box on its side and then putting a bottle right at the back of it," he continued. "Dick and I would have a contest to see

who could break it first. It was quite a trick to drive the
puck into the box hard enough, and at the same time,
there wouldn't be any fragments to clean up because it
would all be in the box."

Now the elder Redmond prefers breaking other
things—like records, for instance. His 52 goals during the
1972-73 National Hockey League campaign set an all-time
Detroit mark for most tallies in a single season. Considering the record was formerly held by the legendary Gordie
Howe, Mickey's milestone is all the more impressive. He
joins such luminaries as Maurice Richard, Bernie Geoff-
rion, Bobby Hull, Johnny Bucyk, and Vic Hadfield—all
of whom have netted 50 goals or more in just one season.

One man who is not surprised at Mickey's exploits is
Red Wings general manager Ned Harkness. It was
Harkness who acquired the youngster, along with forwards
Bill Collins and Guy Charron, from the Montreal Canadiens in 1971 in exchange for superstar Frank Mahovlich.
At the time, Redmond was seeing little action for Montreal, despite scoring 27 goals for the Canadiens in the
previous season. Yet handsome Mickey never expected the
swap.

"It was my first experience at being traded, and I didn't
know how to handle it. First I was pretty upset, but then I
was happy."

The deal was designed to pump some new blood into
the plummeting Wings. Although Frank Mahovlich has
continued to terrorize goalies for the Habs, playing a vital
role on the power play and as a penalty-killer in addition
to a regular shift at left wing, Harkness' move just began
to pay dividends for Detroit last season.

"Our feeling in scouting Redmond," Harkness revealed,
"was that he was the same type of hockey player as
Frank. We needed help on the right side and he gave it to
us. Now I feel that Mickey is as good a right winger as
there is in the league."

Redmond's forte is his overpowering shot, which has
been known to cause opposing goaltenders great distress.
The 5-11, 170-pounder claims he acquired the shot by
practicing with a metal puck while playing Junior A
hockey for the Peterborough Petes.

"It was too heavy to slap," he said. "You had to push it

with a wrist shot. But when I'd get out on the ice with a real rubber puck, it used to feel like I was shooting a twenty-five-cent piece."

Former Detroit coach Johnny Wilson believes there's another explanation for Redmond's scoring prowess.

"It's his strength," Wilson chortled. "He must be the strongest guy in the league. Why, he had the training staff shopping around for extra weights for our gymnasium because the ones we had weren't enough to keep him in shape. They were too light for him."

But Wilson is not totally pleased with the way Redmond relies on his big shot, a factor that no doubt will bother new Red Wings coach Ted Garvin.

"Mickey could score 75 goals a year if he'd develop a little finesse," Wilson lamented. "He thinks he can blast the puck right through people. A lot of times he can, too. But there are also a lot of times when a little shift or a change-up would pay off for him."

Redmond utilized neither power nor finesse to score his 50th goal. Instead he relied on Lady Luck.

"I must admit, I didn't even see the puck," the skillful scorer said after he deflected defenseman Gary Bergman's shot behind Toronto Maple Leaf netminder Ron Low. "I just saw the goalie look behind him and I knew I must have got it."

Although the Red Wings were finally edged out of the fourth and final playoff spot in the East Division last season by the hotshot Buffalo Sabres, it wouldn't surprise anyone if Detroit regrouped in 1974 to once again challenge for The Stanley Cup. According to Wilson and other observers, Mickey Redmond is the key.

"Once he learns the knack of being a little tricky," Wilson explained, "and when he positions himself better on the power play, instead of going in too deep, he'll break all the records there are to break.

SERGE SAVARD In describing Montreal's Stanley Cup champions not long ago, Canadian broadcaster Peter Gzowski pinpointed their distinct quality.

"On the ice," said Gzowski, "the Canadiens swoop and gambol, skating like fury and burning with zeal; they are somehow romantic, like Scaramouche or Cyrano or Jean Gascon."

It is an apt description. All we have to do is substitute a few names like Yvan Cournoyer or Serge Savard.

The last one, Savard, of course, is relatively new to the long and awesome Canadiens Hall of Stars but there is every evidence that the 6-2, 200-pound defenseman will someday be compared with such honored Montreal backliners as Emile "Butch" Bouchard and Ken Reardon, not to mention the finest of them all, Doug Harvey.

He took a giant step toward reaching that revered plateau in September 1972 when he starred for Team Canada in its classic series with the Soviet National Hockey Team. But Montreal hockey fans are more appreciative of his contributions during the 1972-73 campaign and the Canadiens' march to The Stanley Cup last May.

Serge's play was so impressive that onlookers were quick to remind each other that he looked just like the Savard of 1969 when, as a sophomore in the National Hockey League, he paced the Canadiens to The Stanley Cup and overshadowed Bobby Orr to win The Conn Smythe Trophy as the most valuable player in The Cup round.

But a series of crippling injuries not only intervened but threatened to end his career, and it was only after the most recent campaign that Savard once again put together the kind of defensive portfolio that once made him Orr's closest rival as the NHL's top defender. Let's flash back for a moment and recall how Serge rose, fell and rose again.

Savard began assembling his credentials in the 1967-68 season, which was his rookie year. Montreal was up against St. Louis in the Stanley Cup finals. The Canadiens were leading the series 1-0 when the teams met for the second game on the Blues' home rink. A defeat for St. Louis would practically assure its burial.

The teams were tied, 0-0, as the clock ticked past the two minutes mark of the third period. The puck dribbled into the corner of the rink not far from the Blues' net. Claude Provost of the Canadiens was the first to get there. He passed it out front as two Blues attempted to stymie him, but they were a half-second too late.

There was an audible report as the six-ounce hunk of black vulcanized rubber cracked into the stick of Serge Savard. It didn't stay there very long. Maybe two seconds. Then, whammo! Savard shot, and the puck sailed past goalie Glenn Hall. The time was 2:17 and neither team scored again. Montreal captured the game, 1-0, and went on to win the series and The Cup in four straight games.

It was a particularly gratifying goal for Savard. The St. Louis coach was Scotty Bowman and if anyone had a score to settle with Bowman it was the young Montreal native. Curiously, Bowman later was to become Serge's coach in Montreal.

"I played junior hockey for Scotty when he coached the young Canadiens in Montreal," Savard explained. "He used to have me take a cold shower before every game to make sure I was wide awake. Well, now you can tell Scotty I don't need a cold shower to wake up for this game."

If anyone was waking up around the National Hockey League—and taking notice—it was Savard's opponents. They became aware that his long strides, his thudding bodychecks, and his calm in the face of stormy games suggested that he could be an All-Star in a couple of years.

Apparently Montreal's managing director, Sam Pollock, felt the same way. Five years ago Pollock had to choose between Savard and Carol Vadnais, another hulking French-Canadian defenseman with abundant talent. The Habitants were oozing with talent on the backline and

Pollock had to make somebody available in the draft. He finally selected Vadnais, who has proven a capable player for Boston. But, then again, Savard has been more than capable for the Canadiens. However, there were times in past seasons when Serge wasn't quite sure about his future.

"The first half of the season," Savard said, "I hardly played at all. It was a strange feeling. You go out for one turn but you can't tell if the coach is going to put you out again. So you start worrying. One mistake and you're through for the night."

Serge managed to get on the ice plenty during the 1968-69 season. He scored eight goals and 23 assists for a total of 31 points. It was a respectable but not especially commanding figure: below the likes of Gilles Marotte and Gary Bergman but above Jim Dorey and Dallas Smith, to give you a better idea of the company he was keeping.

When a Montreal writer dared suggest that Savard might someday be in a class with Bobby Orr, D. Leo Monahan of the *Boston Record-American* made it abundantly clear that *that* would be the day when Savard could carry Orr's shoes.

Leo was right, until the Canadiens entered the first round of the East Division's Stanley Cup playoff against the New York Rangers. All of a sudden Savard became a commanding figure, lugging the puck on long rink-length dashes, playing the stout defensive game, and looking like a man who would never need a cold shower to awaken him.

The Canadiens dispatched the Rangers in four straight games and now they were ready for the ultimate test. The game against the Bruins would not only decide the East Division champions but also the Stanley Cup winner because everybody knew that the series against the West finalist would be a routine gag.

Montreal won the opening game, 3-2, in sudden death overtime on the home Forum ice, but even the staunchest backers of the Flying Frenchmen were willing to concede they were lucky to scrape out on Ralph Backstrom's sudden death goal. The second game at The Forum would be the big test.

Midway in the second period, Savard took the ice on a penalty-killing assignment for the Canadiens. The puck was free behind the Montreal net. Savard skated to it, gathered it in on the blade of his stick and began moving out toward the front of the net and goalie Gump Worsley.

It was a time to ice the puck out of danger. Or at the very least to pass it off to a free teammate. It was *not* the time or the place to put on a stickhandling exhibition for the home folks.

But that's exactly what Savard proposed to do.

He had accomplished about five feet and two seconds' worth of performance when Johnny Bucyk of the Bruins swooped down on him, relieved Serge of the puck, and skimmed it across to teammate John McKenzie, who took two swings and finally lifted the rubber past Worsley.

It was a classic dum-dum play. What matters is that even Bouchard, Harvey, and Reardon have done likewise in their day. And they recovered from the *faux pas.* Savard's mettle would be tested in the minutes to come. The twenty-four-year-old was not yanked out of the game by his coach, Claude Ruel, which was the first key turning point. Savard came on for the next shift and the one after that *and* the one after that.

The Canadiens were trailing by a goal late in the third period. Very late, in fact. Less than two minutes were remaining when Savard saved the Canadiens, the way he saved them with a few key passes in the opening game against Boston.

Montreal organized a massive five-man attack against the Bruin goal but it failed. The Boston offensive unit quickly counterattacked against the temporarily abandoned goalie Gump Worsley. But Savard somehow speeded back and deftly intercepted a pass from Phil Esposito to Ken Hodge.

Once again play was turned in the direction of the Boston zone. This time the puck went from Yvan Cournoyer to Savard who lifted the disk past goalie Ed Johnston's flying right pad and into the corner of the net. Significantly, Bobby Orr was sprawled on his hands and knees at the moment Savard tied the score. Only 69 seconds remained in the period when the red light went on.

"You've got to get a break to do something like that,"

said Savard. "It was good to get a goal. I figured the first Boston goal was my fault when I tried to carry the puck out instead of shooting it down the ice."

Now the game went into sudden death overtime, and Bruin defenseman Ted Green rapidly took a two-minute penalty for holding when the Canadiens cranked up their power play deep in Bruin territory.

Backstrom won the decisive face-off from Ed Westfall in the left circle; the puck moved immediately behind Backstrom to John Ferguson, who sent it all the way behind him to the far left blue line, where Savard attacked the disk and sent it orbiting toward the Boston net. Mickey Redmond of the Canadiens was standing in front of the goal when Savard shot.

"I had my stick on the ice where it's supposed to be," said Redmond.

Sure enough, Savard's drive caromed off Redmond's blade and zoomed crazily into the air and past the befuddled Johnston. And, so, Savard helped win another game.

So after two games Savard could boast that a) he had set up all three Montreal goals in the opening match, b) tied the game in the second contest and, c) assisted on the sudden death winner in the second game. Suddenly, critics began noticing the young man coach Ruel had been touting all along.

"Serge is an example of the competitive spirit you need in the playoffs," said Ruel. "It is impossible to demand more from him than he has given since the start of the season."

The kudos weren't limited to the Montreal observers either. Harold Kaese, sports columnist of the *Boston Globe*, singled out Savard as the top man in the series.

"Savard," wrote Red MacLeod, the distinguished writer with the *Toronto Globe and Mail*, "has matured as one of the Canadiens' more accomplished players in the playoffs."

Boston rebounded to win the next two games, 5-0 and 3-2. Savard scored Montreal's second goal in the 3-2 game with 54 seconds remaining and showed no signs of diminishing talent.

The Canadiens then returned home to The Forum, trimmed Boston 4-2, and set the stage for the sixth and what proved to be the final game of the series at Boston Garden.

The Bruins took a 1-0 lead on a goal by Ron Murphy early in the game and held on to it with great tenacity through the second period and into the third. But Bruin defenseman Don Awrey took a penalty at 1:05 of the period and the Canadiens' power play went into action again. Captain Jean Beliveau started the play by ladling a pass to Savard at the right point. His long shot sailed toward goalie Gerry Cheevers who happened to be screened by Orr. The puck flew past him and it was a new hockey game. The Canadiens went on to win it in double overtime on a goal by Beliveau.

That set the stage for the Stanley Cup final between St. Louis and Montreal. Nobody expected the Blues to win at The Forum—they blew the first two games by 3-1 scores—but the West Division champs were thought to have a chance in the third game of the series at their own St. Louis Arena, jammed with a record crowd of 16,338 on Thursday night, 1 May 1969.

The score was 0-0 in the first period when Dick Duff of the Canadiens passed the puck to Savard who was astride the St. Louis blue line. "When the Blues' defense opened up," Savard explained, "I kept skating until I was about three strides over the line. One of their defensemen came over to form a partial screen and I let the shot go. I think maybe Jacques Plante saw it too late."

Whether he saw it or not is irrelevant. The puck was in and the Canadiens were off and skating to a 4-0 victory, giving the Canadiens a 3-0 lead in the series. They wrapped it up on 4 May with a 2-1 win and a four-game sweep of the Cup finale for the second year in a row.

Throughout the Cup finals speculation was rife over which Montreal player would skate off with the Conn Smythe Trophy as the most valuable player in the Stanley Cup playoffs. Beliveau, Dick Duff, Rogatien Vachon were all candidates but the favorite remained Savard. Serge confirmed the thinking by becoming the first defenseman ever to win the prize.

He was at the apex of his young career and then, just as suddenly, everything went wrong. Late in the 1969-70 season he suffered a fractured left leg. It was a serious break and his return was delayed several times because doctors feared for the slow healing process. When he did come back in the 1970-71 campaign the leg was refractured in January 1971. This time Serge underwent a delicate bone-grafting operation in February 1971 and missed the beginning of the 1971-72 campaign, so that he might recuperate completely.

His turnabout on the road back to the top came in September 1972, when he became a member of Team Canada. "I didn't realize it at the time," said Savard, "but it was going to take months and months of work during the 1972-73 season before I got back into top shape."

Gradually, he rounded into his 1969 form, and in March 1973 he wore a large grin as the Canadiens annexed first-place in the East. "The best thing that happened to me," he recalled, "was winning the division so early. That gave me time to relax and build myself up again. After all, I had been playing steadily for eight months."

He finished the season with seven goals and 32 assists for 39 points and explained that maturity had made him "more of a defenseman now" than he had been in his youth.

At twenty-seven years, Serge is approaching the prime of his playing career. His teammates realized that when, after he sipped champagne from The Stanley Cup last May, he laughed and said, "I feel like I did back in 1969!"

PAT STAPLETON Midway in the Stanley Cup semi-final round between the New York Rangers and Chicago Black Hawks last April, Chicago manager Tommy Ivan was asked whether there's still room for "a good little man" in big-league hockey.

Ivan nearly leaped out of his brogues in anger at the question. "You won't find a better 'little man' playing defense than the guy wearing number twelve on our team."

Number Twelve, Pat Stapleton, stands 5-7 and weighs 180 pounds. Playing against giants such as Peter Mahovlich 6-4, 210 pounds, the defenseman called "Whitey" looks like a Lilliputian. But his contribution to Chicago's march to the 1973 Stanley Cup final was less surprising than his jump to the WHA Chicago Cougars as Player Coach.

"Few National Hockey League defensemen have been superior to Stapleton over the past eight seasons," said *Toronto Star* sports editor Jim Proudfoot.

The thirty-three-year-old native of Sarnia, Ontario, joins a distinguished line of smallish defensemen who have starred down through the years. King Clancy, who performed for the Toronto Maple Leafs in the thirties, was the best of the pre-war era while Pierre Pilote, who skated for Chicago's last Stanley Cup-winner in 1961, was a more recent lighthorse type who reached the top. Then, along came Whitey in the fall of 1965, when Pilote suffered a serious hand injury.

"Up until that time I was going nowhere," Pat asserted. "That was the turning point in my career. When Pilote got hurt, I took his place on the power play and when he returned we shared the power play assignments."

From that point until May 1973 Stapleton proved his claim to stardom. He was in on 327 goals and earned All-Star recognition three times. It was a remarkable turn-around for a young man who had previously thought he was too small for hockey and, perhaps, too inept. What turned it all around for him was a good education in the minor leagues.

He had played junior hockey in St. Catherines, Ontario, and turned pro in 1960 with Sault Sainte Marie. In 1961-62 he moved right up to the NHL when the Boston Bruins drafted him but Pat was smart enough to realize that that was a Pyrrhic victory.

"The Bruins had a terrible team then," said Stapleton, "and I never played very well. I really began to wonder if I was too small to be in the NHL. After all, if I couldn't play for the Bruins, who could I play for?"

Boston finally dispatched him to Portland of the Western League where ex-Bruins defenseman Hal Laycoe

was coach and manager. A professional type, Laycoe gave
Stapleton just the kind of lessons he needed to restore his
confidence and improve his game.

"Laycoe got me to play about ten pounds lighter," said
Pat, "and at 180 pounds, I found that I was able to move
a step quicker. I was able to keep up with the speedy guys
like Willie O'Ree. On top of that, Hal gave me confidence,
which I badly needed after the Boston experience."

One of the primary lessons was that you don't have to
be gigantic to be a good defenseman. "I had always tried
to muscle people," said Stapleton. "Before I got to Portland, whenever I tried the muscle technique it failed. In
Portland I learned how to finesse them, how to box them
away from the goal without getting run over."

After two seasons in Portland he was voted the WHL's
best defenseman and was ready for bigger and better
things. That's where the Bruins and the Toronto Maple
Leafs made major mistakes. They both figured that Pat
still wasn't capable enough for the majors.

Following his excellent second season in Portland, Pat
was traded by the Bruins to Toronto along with Orland
Kurtenbach and Andy Hebenton for Ron Stewart. When
Pat arrived in Toronto he discovered that the Maple
Leafs' defense corps was bulging with solid players. The
Toronto brass decided to leave Pat unprotected in the
draft and he was immediately claimed by Tommy Ivan in
Chicago.

At first it appeared that the Black Hawks were going to
overlook him, too. "They tried me out as a right defenseman," said Pat, "and it hampered me." He was dispatched
to St. Louis of the Central League and played 14 minor
league games before being recalled as a left defenseman.
He never played in the minors again.

"I was surprised that he did so well when we recalled
him," said Chicago coach Billy Reay. "There's no secret
that a good big man is better than a good little man. On
the other hand, a good little man is better than a fair big
man. He's short all right, but he is strong."

Once Whitey became a Black Hawks regular, Chicago
enjoyed the most consistent run of winners in its long
hockey history. In April 1967 the Black Hawks finished
first for the first time ever. Between 1967 and 1973 Chi-

cago finished first five out of seven tries and Pat was rewarded with the captaincy of the club. However, the "C" was removed from his jersey three years ago following a salary dispute and his relationship with the Black Hawks' front office remained abrasive through the 1972-73 campaign, resulting in his defection to the WHA.

At one point last season Reay inexplicably benched Stapleton. He was returned to the lineup only after the club faltered and veteran Stan Mikita openly blasted the Hawks' front office for allowing Pat to vegetate on the bench. Once Whitey returned to the lineup the Hawks marched on to the Clarence Campbell Bowl, emblematic of the West Division championship.

He reached the pinnacle of his success in the 1973 playoffs. Chicago easily wiped out St. Louis in the opening round but the Hawks were expected to be clobbered by a strong Rangers sextet in the semi-finals. Instead, the Chicago defense, headed by Stapleton and his tobacco-chewing partner, Bill White, frustrated the Rangers to the point where the New York offense disintegrated before the astonished Broadway Blues.

"Finding the puck was never any problem," said Rangers captain Vic Hadfield. "Stapleton always had it. Trouble was, we couldn't get it away from him." One of Hadfield's teammates put it another way: "We completed more passes to Stapleton than to any of our own guys."

Thanks to Pat's performance, the Black Hawks upset the Rangers four games to one and advanced to the Cup finals against Montreal's mighty Canadiens. "If Stapleton plays against Montreal the way he played against us," said Rangers manager-coach Emile Francis, "Chicago will win The Stanley Cup."

Stapleton was as ubiquitous as ever but the Canadiens would not be denied, although Chicago did give them a scare. With Montreal leading three games to one, Chicago bounced back to score an astonishing 8-7 victory at the Montreal Forum.

"I've never experienced a night like it," said Stapleton. "I made some rotten plays and then something would work nicely and I'd be congratulating myself. Then I'd louse something up. It was a nightmare with a happy ending. Somebody told me I alternated between terrible and wonderful."

But Chicago prevailed and one critic pointed at Whitey and his partner for the credit. "Stapleton atoned for his miscues in the final eight minutes of the game when he and White actually enabled the Hawks to control proceedings and protect a one-goal edge which, the way things had been going, seemed awfully precarious."

Unfortunately for Pat, the Canadiens rallied in the sixth game and beat his Black Hawks at Chicago Stadium for The Cup. Was Whitey depressed? Sure, but not for long. He knows that he's too good not to come up a winner.

"The wheel always turns," he reasoned. "One day you're on the bottom, the next morning you're on top. My day on top will be coming soon with the Cougars!"

STEVE VICKERS The 1973 Stanley Cup quarterfinal series between the New York Rangers and Boston Bruins was all over but the shouting. For most of the Broadway Blueshirts, who had suffered through years of frustration and humiliation at the hands of the Bostonians, a little gloating and general hell-raising was in order. They had just eliminated the Bruins in five games. The clincher, a 6-3 win, coming on Boston's home ice.

But off in a corner of the Ranger locker room sat Steve Vickers, the author of three of the New Yorkers' six goals and the man who soon would be named rookie-of-the-year.

"I knew we could beat Boston, but what surprises me is that it was this easy," Vickers said in his typically casual manner.

Yes, Steve, but your hat trick. How did it feel for a rookie to score a three-goal hat trick in the Stanley Cup playoffs?

"Terrific."

Terrific? Just terrific? Could it be that Steve was putting people on with his offhand attitude?

"No, he's not just pretending," assured teammate Brad Park when asked about Vickers' aloofness. "He's really that way. He just shrugs things off."

It seems that the enigmatic Vickers really is that way. For a couple of weeks earlier in the 1972-73 season, the Ranger rookie left wing was the hottest name around the Fun City sports pages. In fact, when the youngster electrified Madison Square Garden patrons with two consecutive hat tricks, he was the biggest news item in all of hockey.

Bold headlines all over New York proclaimed *"VICKERS MAKES HISTORY"* and *"VICKERS SHOOTING LIKE BOBBY HULL!!!"* With that kind of press, no one could have faulted any twenty-two-year-old Toronto native for walking with his head in the clouds.

But not Steve Vickers. When he was asked about his scoring splurge, the quiet, introspective young man refused to claim credit.

"Walter Tkaczuk just shoveled me the puck and I poked it in." Or, "Billy (Fairbairn) put me in the clear with a perfect pass."

And on and on. For each goal Steve scored he downplayed his own role while heaping praise on his teammates, although he eventually won the rookie award.

"Maybe he doesn't make much noise in the locker room, but he's sure been causing some noise out there on the ice," boasted Ranger manager Emile Francis.

The noise out on the ice resembled a sonic boom when Vickers literally burst onto the scene. On November 12, just two games after he was inserted on the left wing with Walter Tkaczuk and Bill Fairbairn, Vickers put three pucks past goaltender Gary Edwards in a 5-1 Ranger win over the Los Angeles Kings.

The very next game he duplicated that effort. This time the victims were the Philadelphia Flyers and their rookie goalkeeper, Michel Belhumeur, as the Rangers skated to a 7-3 romp.

Vickers' feat of consecutive hat tricks sent hockey writers scurrying off in all directions checking the record books. When the typewriters had stopped clicking, Steve emerged as the only Ranger, rookie or otherwise, to ever tip the hat in consecutive contests. No rookie had ever done it in NHL history.

Drafted number one by the Rangers from the Toronto Marlboros in 1971, Vickers was a lefty shooting right winger. Playing on the Marlboros' second line (Islander Billy Harris played on the first), Steve scored 43 goals and 107 points for the Marlies in his last season with them. Assigned to the Omaha Knights of the Central League in 1971-72, Steve was switched to the port side and responded with 36 goals and 59 points.

The following Fall, at the Ranger training camp in Kitchener, Steve was out to prove that he could play in the NHL. He knew that he was in for a fight if he wanted to make the trip south to New York. The Rangers had the flashy Gene Carr, the incumbent left wing on the Tkaczuk line, and two other highly touted candidates for that spot, rookie Tom Williams and Curt Bennett, a former All-America at Brown.

"All I heard last summer was Gene Carr, Curt Bennett and Tommy Williams," Steve recalled. "It helped me push that much harder in training camp to make this club."

Skating mostly with Tkaczuk and Fairbairn, Vickers quietly impressed Francis and the talent-laden Rangers. The manager summed up the feeling: "He just played so well and so consistently that we had to keep him."

For Vickers, a kid with only one year of pro experience, making the big club with a Stanley Cup contender must have been overwhelming, wasn't it?

"No, not really," was his confident, yet low-keyed reply. "I had a good year at Omaha and I worked out during the summer to get an extra good start."

Vickers' heroics continued after the two three-goal performances. In the Rangers' very next game, against the St. Louis Blues, Steve netted the game-winner and also assisted on the final goal in a 3-1 Ranger win. As it turned out, that was to be the last goal from Vickers for at least a while.

The Rangers returned from St. Louis to face the Pittsburgh Penguins at Madison Square Garden the following evening. During the third period, Vickers came out of a tangle with defenseman Darryl Edestrand with strained ligaments in his left knee. Sidelined for 16 games, Vickers was somewhat depressed, but his cool exterior never shattered.

"That's the way it goes sometimes," he philosophized, "there's no use getting worked up over something you can't do anything about."

Upon his return from the injury, however, Vickers resumed his scoring as if he had never been gone. Establishing himself as the regular left wing on the Tkaczuk line, Steve and his linemates almost singlehandedly demolished the Bruins at Boston Garden.

Despite his enforced absence, Vickers completed his rookie season with 30 goals and 23 assists for 53 points. He also emerged as the New Yorkers' most accurate shooter, finishing the season with a 22.9 shooting percentage, or better than a goal for every five shots.

Steve's instant success was due to his grittiness in the corners and absolute refusal to be moved from the opposition's crease. Making his own breaks, he scored most of his goals from tip-ins, rebounds, or scrambles in front of the net. His slapshot, however, is more than adequate and he is quick to pull the trigger when he has the opening for the shot.

Vickers' weaknesses are in his passing game and his speed, but he has impressed the Ranger management with his two-way playing and vigilant patrolling of his wing.

"He skates up and down his wing like a vet," observed Francis about a quality that perhaps gave Vickers the edge over the more free-wheeling Gene Carr.

Not one to shy away from even the toughest men in the league, Vickers scoffs at suggestions that he may emerge as the rugged type needed as a team policeman. Yet, he has squared off with such rugged types as André Dupont, Bob Stewart, and Don Marcotte, the latter being a knockdown-dragout affair in Boston Garden with Vickers the unanimous winner by a knockdown.

"I set certain levels for myself as a rookie," Vickers explained. "My first objective was to play regularly. The second was scoring twenty goals."

The rookie-of-the-year award was not in the original plans, but The Calder Trophy didn't surprise him either.

RON WARD It simply did not make sense.

There was center Ron Ward, who had scored a grand total of two goals in 71 National Hockey League games with Vancouver in 1971-72, sitting rather comfortably in second place in the World Hockey Association scoring list last April with 51 goals, 67 assists for 118 points.

And there you have the hockey story of 1972-73. Almost from the very start, Ron Ward was the WHA's top point man, until he was beaten out by Andre Lacroix in the last week of the season.

It borders on the unbelievable not because of his goals or his assists, or the fact that Ward had made the New York Raiders an occasionally impressive hockey club but mostly because he never wanted to be a forward in the first place.

"When I joined the Raiders," said the articulate Ward, "I wanted more than anything to play defense. Somehow I always had the notion that I'd be a good defenseman and never got the chance with Toronto or Vancouver in the NHL."

Raiders' coach Camille Henry was a flexible fellow. Against his better judgment, he figured, "If Ron Ward wants to be a defenseman, I'll let him."

"Actually," said Henry, "I knew in my heart that Ron should be a center. I knew it in my mind, too, because I had seen him play center for Tulsa in the Central League when I was coaching Kansas City. It was obvious that he knew how to score goals—and set them up, too."

But, being a nice guy, Henry let Ward have his way at the Raiders' training camp in September 1972. Ron played adequately behind the blue line, but a Bobby Orr he was not. But he has brains and, more than most, he is a team man.

"After a week or so," Ward explained, "I realized that

we were hurting at center because Garry Peters was out with his knee trouble, and we were pretty strong on defense. I figured I could help up front."

Right off the stick, this 5-11, 175-pound native of Cornwall, Ontario, found the inside of the net. And by December he had savored nine multiple-goal games, including the fastest World Hockey Association hat-trick—three goals in six minutes and 44 seconds on 29 November 1972 against New England.

Ministerial looking and intense in his approach to the game, Ward packs an old-time wrist shot that works better than his slapper, and he uses his head more than most.

"I was at the Maple Leafs' camp in the fall of 1969," Ward recalled of one of the brief tryouts he had with NHL teams, "and had a really good training season. They had me at center and, if I'm not mistaken, I finished second in scoring behind Norm Ullman and ahead of fellows like Dave Keon and Ron Ellis."

Until recently, when Ward would be asked why he didn't make it in Toronto, he'd say it was a matter of "politics." This time he amplified:

"We were close to finishing one of our workouts and I had been skating hard and was beat. I happened to be leaning against the sideboards when this chap leaned over and made some remarks about how I could be a better player. I was in no mood to hear any cracks like that so I told him to get away from me, or words to that effect.

"Since I had never been one to mingle with the big shots on any team, I had no idea that the man I had told off was the president of the team, Stafford Smythe!"

Suddenly, the productive center discovered that he no longer was given the ice time that had enabled him to score so easily in training camp. Not long after that, according to Ward, Leafs Coach John McLellan told people that there was a skater on his team he would have liked to use—but couldn't.

"It wasn't fair at all," Ron asserted. "I just sat on the bench, and watched and watched. Finally, I went to Jim Gregory the manager, and told him I wanted to play. He kept telling me to wait and wait, but nothing ever happened."

In June, 1970, Ward's shackles were released by the

Vancouver Canucks, who drafted him from Toronto. At least, now he thought, he would be free to strut his stuff. The Canucks sent him to Rochester of the American League for a season, but elevated him to the NHL last year.

"My luck," he went on, "the Canucks had lots of centers; guys like Orland Kurtenbach and André Boudrias. Maybe I was my own worst enemy by doing it, but I told Bud Poile [the Canucks' general manager] that I came to play."

The Canuck high command was not impressed. Ward was told straight out that he would never be a regular. So he killed penalties and more penalties and wound up with two goals and four assists over a full season.

The Canucks wound up in a relatively dismal place in the standings, a situation that should at least have inspired Poile to try Ward in 1972-73 on a more regular basis. When the WHA Raiders made Ron an offer, he suggested to the Canucks that now was the time for them to assert their confidence in him. They replied that he was destined to be a penalty-killer so he said thank you and good-bye.

Ironically, he was signed in New York City amid a bulging press conference called to hail the arrival of Alton White, who supposedly would be the Raiders' big attraction because he was the only black in the WHA.

"Who is that guy with Alton White?" was the question asked when Ron posed with the Negro stickhandler, helping slice the cake on White's twenty-seventh birthday.

By December 1972 White had been a forgotten man on Broadway and was traded to Los Angeles while Ward emerged as the most regal of the Raiders. He didn't let it go to his head, though.

Here's a good for-instance: because of his limited scoring in 1971-72, Ron did not receive what you would call a healthy goal-scoring bonus from the Raider management. But there was a bonus and he reached it long before Christmas 1972.

Instead of pocketing all of the money, he wrote a check for $200 and gave it to the Raiders' assistant trainer, Tom Fitzgerald.

"Tom's not making that much money," said Ward, with

obvious embarrassment when the episode was mentioned. "What the heck—I've been lucky, so why shouldn't I let him in on it?"

The Raiders also were fortunate that Ward collected some much-needed ink for their box office. A national wire service profiled him and *Sports Illustrated* did likewise with the title "The Garbage Man Cometh." He was amused by the label, especially since his coach had long been renowned for his garbage goals in the NHL.

"Yes," Ron agreed, "I am a garbage-collector but the puck goes in, and when the red light goes on, it counts like the most beautiful goal ever scored."

One thing he is not is a fighter. Ron traces his peacemaking instincts to his early hockey learning at a religious junior high school he attended near Cornwall.

"Fighting was forbidden," said Ward. "Besides, I never like to fight. I've learned to be able to take a stick in the mouth or a butt-end in the ribs and keep on playing. Maybe that's why I take so much in the pros; and, personally, I think I'm a bigger man for it.

"My personal theory on hockey fighting is that, for me, it's not the thing to do to my opponent or to myself because I'm afraid that I might hurt him, or he might hurt me."

Besides learning that at the religous school, Ward gained a wide knowledge of hockey fundamentals. Every day during a fifteen-minute recess the coach would put the boys through a vigorous exercise in wrist-shooting the puck. Slapping was verboten.

"Now," said Coach Henry, "his shot is not hard but really heavy. By that I mean that a goalkeeper will see it coming and think it will stay in the same flight pattern. Then, all of a sudden, it will take off like a baseball pitcher's slider and the goalie will miss it completely."

Those childhood practices also enabled Ward to obtain a radar-like knowledge of the goal area no matter where he might be located on the ice.

"Somehow, I've learned to shoot the puck without knowing where the net is and be able to score on a good percentage of those shots," Ron said.

That's why he felt so frustrated in the Vancouver and

Toronto organizations and why last season had been so gratifying.

"A lot of players give 100 per cent," he said. "My policy has been to give 110 per cent whenever I can. That's why it was so sickening to go four years without being on a winner, until now.

"Last season things got so good—I never dreamed it possible. I didn't want to say too much because I was afraid everything would suddenly backfire on me."

Well, maybe it will and maybe it won't. Ron bought a house in suburban Verona, New Jersey, and moved in with his family—wife Patty and the girls, Brigette, six, and Shannon, one year and eight months. Then he was traded to Vancouver Blazers.

"Imagine," Ward said, in the fall of 1972 "I was really down when I came to New York. Everything had gone wrong. The baby was sick, we couldn't find a house and I just got fed up. Finally, I told them, 'Trade me—I wanna get out of here.' But the Raiders were patient. Marvin Milkes and Herb Elk [then general manager and assistant general manager] took good care of me and things straightened out. Then they up and traded me."

In time Ward will have his B.A. degree from Ottawa University and then will begin law studies. "It's funny," he said. "When I was seventeen-years-old I played junior hockey for the Oshawa Generals. One day a fourteen-year-old kid joined the team. His name was Bobby Orr. Up until that time I had dreamed that someday I'd be the best hockey player in the world. After seeing Orr, I said I'd settle for second best. Then, along came Phil Esposito. Eventually I said, maybe I'll be 100th best.

"Now, who knows?"

THE OTHER HOCKEYS, 1974

THE STREET HOCKEY SCENE
BY MIKE RUBIN

WHEN it comes to expansion and planning for the future, Don Rocci, President of the Northeast Street Hockey League, is certainly no slouch.

"After last season," Don recalled, "we figured that expanding to cities outside of Massachusetts would make our league sort of special. We got in touch with a representative of what used to be the New York City Street Hockey League, and decided to merge."

So while the National Hockey League annexed franchises in Atlanta and Long Island, and the infant World Hockey Association struggled to provide big-league shinny in a dozen cities across North America, the Northeast Street Hockey League hatched the New York Division. The brand new circuit boasted entries from colleges and universities all around the New York City area—Hofstra University, Brooklyn College, Yeshiva University, Brooklyn Polytechnic Institute, Jewish Theological Seminary, and, of course, Columbia University, 1972 City League champs and the place where street hockey made its Metropolitan debut.

In 1973 the Lions of Columbia once again finished first in their division, sporting an enviable 12-3 record and baptizing several new teams in the process. The toughest competition came from a squad representing Shippensburg State College in Pennsylvania. The two clubs played a home-and-home series, with Columbia taking the first two contests and Shippensburg rallying to win the third. Shippensburg captain Mike Helm predicts more of the latter results in the future.

Just what is this sport called street hockey? To begin with, the object of the game is the same as in ice hockey—to put the puck in the net—only a ball is commonly used in place of the hard-rubber disc, and card-

board boxes, trash cans, or bicycles are often substituted
for the customary iron pipes and thick twine goals.

Street hockey can be played on virtually any hard,
wide-open area. Actually, the term "street" is often a
misnomer, since many teams prefer to play on a gym floor
or other indoor surface.

Each player is equipped with either a regular wooden
hockey stick or a special street hockey stick with a plastic
blade. Originally developed by Mylec, Inc., a sporting
goods manufacturer located in western Massachusetts, the
plastic blade, which can be screwed onto the shaft of any
old broken stick, revolutionized the game of street hockey.
Youngsters no longer had to spend a small fortune on
wooden sticks that would inevitably splinter during the
course of a game. The plastic blades wear down slowly
and smoothly when used on a rough cement-like surface,
and almost never break.

In addition to the plastic blade, Mylec has invented a
number of other practical and inexpensive pieces of street
hockey equipment, like balls, pucks, and various types of
protective padding, that have served to enhance the sport.
Mylec president, Raymond Leclerc, contends that these
equipment developments are of immeasurable value to the
game.

"We believe," Leclerc asserted, "that our equipment will
eventually elevate the image of street hockey to a point
where it will be more generally accepted as an organized
sport."

Another man who has done a lot to encourage organization in street hockey is William Cohen, a Boston sales-
man. During the fall of 1971, Cohen founded the National
Street Hockey Association to promote the establishment of
regional street hockey leagues, with the NSHA acting as a
central authority. But Cohen's organization is more than
just a commissioner's office.

"Our primary purpose in creating the NSHA," Cohen
revealed, "was to encourage safety and sportsmanship in
street hockey by helping kids set up official leagues. We
publish a quarterly newsletter, and for the membership fee
of two dollars, a youngster gets a subscription to the paper
plus a membership card, decals, an informative handbook,
and liberal discounts on NSHA-sponsored events.

"In addition," Cohen continued, "we hold a semi-annual tournament in Boston. All teams belonging to the NSHA are eligible to compete, and I think it's fair to say that our three tournaments so far have been resounding successes. In addition we have an insurance program which any member of the NSHA can elect to join. The cost is very reasonable and the protection is complete. And we hope to make equipment available to our members at reduced rates in the near future."

For further information regarding the National Street Hockey Association, you can write to William Cohen at 44 Farnsworth Street, Boston, Massachusetts 02210.

What's in store for street hockey in the near future? Further expansion, for one thing. The game has already spread to most NHL cities and is flourishing in Sweden, Denmark, Finland, and the Netherlands. According to Mylec, Switzerland and West Germany are probable markets for 1974. In short, the game's appeal knows no bounds.

Next stop—the Soviet Union! And then . . . well, would you believe the World Cup of Street Hockey?!

TABLE HOCKEY AT THE SUMMIT

BY STAN ISAACS, Sports Editor, Newsday, Long Island, New York

Reprinted by permission from **Newsday**, 1973

WHICH is the deeper experience? Watching Bobby Orr, the hockey player, or being Bobby Orr, hockey player? David Feinberg and Mark Abkowitz of Boston will affirm it is more rewarding to be a Bobby Orr.

Feinberg and Abkowitz are the pair who emerged triumphant in the 1973 World Table Hockey Association Doubles Tournament. They worked their feverish fingers over a table hockey board for nine hours of day-and-evening play and emerged with the coveted T. J. Rugg Cup in February, 1973.

The World Table Hockey Association Tournament is in the forefront of the movement to push sport beyond the frontier of mere spectator experience. The tournament is for those in the grandstand who want to climb down into the arena and savor the thrill of battle for themselves. Table hockey is the board game that emulates ice hockey, with little metal men banging a wooden puck to a fare-theewell at a little metal goalie, who, in the hands of a WTHA ace, more often than not turns away the shot.

World Table Hockey Tournament play started four years ago in the upper west side New York apartment of founder Stan Fischler, gadfly of the hockey press corps. The tournament was a hit to the extent it overflowed into a seedy hotel in downtown Manhattan two years ago. On 13 February 1973 it was moved uptown to a ballroom atop the Statler Hilton.

The entry list included colorfully-clad teams from Minneapolis, Chicago, Toronto, and Montreal as well as a contingent of stalwart New Yorkers. Fischler helped round out the field with eccentrics, including newspapermen and celebrity athletes. Among them were Jim Bouton, football player Randy Vataha, and an ex-hockey player named Larry Zeidel who stormed out of the hotel ballroom in disgust after allowing a deciding goal in a key game. Zeidel came to play but he did not come to lose.

People with a keen understanding of triumph and tragedy laughed; the players grimaced. The Minnesota Crows, the defending champions, smoked like fishes during the pre-tournament greetings by chairman Bob Stampleman. It was no surprise to keen analysts that the nervous Minnesota twins lost their first match and were never serious contenders.

Among the crowd favorites were the Montreals, who called themselves Team Canada. They wore special T-shirts modeled after the shirts worn by Canada's national team last summer against the Russians. Team Canada included two players and a manager; he charted shots on goals and saves during play.

The early rounds were enlivened, as ever, by Neil

Shayne, the man who failed to land a World Hockey Association franchise in the Nassau Coliseum. Shayne, a Philadelphia lawyer from Woodmere, broke his own record by filing six protests in the first five minutes of tournament play.

Controversy raged over the poor quality of the boards used in the tournament. As the rate of board breakdowns increased, the manufacturer's man, who was sent to act as tournament mechanic—departed. He said he had to take a plane to Germany.

The Bostons won by beating Chicago's Dean Muench and Rick Sorci in the best-of-three finals, 1-2, 5-4, 5-2. The winners stunned the crowd with effective use of a jump shot by their right defenseman which unerringly sailed over the shoulder of the enemy goalie. The Bostons survived heated rooting against them because the telecast of the rough Boston-Rangers' game was piped into the tournament. They will return to defend their title when the 1974 singles and doubles World Championships are held in New York in February 1974.

The WTHA tournament has been shown on United States and Canadian television. The man who produced the half-hour special for Canada's CBC is so celebrated in his land that he once was hired to stage a bar mitzvah by a proud father in Toronto. The event was such an extravaganza, the guest had a great time, but the father was invited to leave the temple.

The WTHA event is so much on its way to becoming a fixture, the board of governors is listening to bids by various organizations that want to sponsor succeeding tournaments. It's founder Fischler dreams that some day the WTHA action will be piped into Madison Square Garden during a Boston-Rangers game.

ART IN HOCKEY
BY SHIRLEY FISCHLER

THERE was Wayne Cashman jolting Reggie Fleming along the boards. Ted Green flailed a fist at Orland Kurtenbach, while crushing a referee between them. From a distance, goalies Lorne "Gump" Worsley and Ed Giacomin stood poised in front of their respective nets. And all the while Derek Sanderson sailed madly around the rink, his stick held high.

A game at Madison Square Garden? No. An All-Star game in Toronto? Wrong again. Give up?

All of these National Hockey League and World Hockey Association skaters are depicted in the unique paintings of Manhattan artist Mary Jo Schwalbach.

"Four summers ago I had an action photograph of Ted Green," said the Wisconsin-born painter, "and suddenly I felt like making a painting of it. I found the parts of an old work and just started reforming. I really don't know how I got the idea."

Mary Jo is not strictly a painter. Her work is perhaps best described as "assemblage"—a bizarre melding-together of wood, cloth, sticks, pucks, glass, string, net, glue, and paint into a three-dimensional picture.

The overall effect is joltingly real and often amusing. In one rounded, bulging action portrait the hockey sticks (obtained from the Ranger dressing room after games at Madison Square Garden) jut a full two feet out of the heavy wooden background of the painting.

And in the Sanderson work, his skates (real children's skates) overhang several inches, making him jump realistically out of the rink background. The audience, incidentally, is made from photographs of real, living hockey figures.

Ms. Schwalbach has had quite a success with her hockey art. Several pieces have shown in a prestigious Madison Avenue gallery and elsewhere. Three works are hanging in the Spectrum in Philadelphia and a family member of New York Rangers' President William Jennings acquired one for his home. Several others have been sold to fans, and the Sabres' Roger Crozier is currently tending goal in a Buffalo bank, Schwalbach style!

One of the Philadelphia paintings—an abstract of a Flyer skating with the puck—caused somewhat of a scene when it was first shown in the Executive Lounge at the Spectrum several seasons ago. Flyers' Chairman Ed Snider was giving then-coach Keith Allen (now general manager) a tour of the new acquisitions, when Allen noticed that the "ice" in the work was actually made of cracked mirror. Allen recoiled in horror, protesting that the broken mirror would bring the Flyers bad luck.

"I only resolved the dilemma," laughed Mary Jo, "after I explained that since I had broken the mirror, I would have the bad luck, not the Flyers."

Mary Jo has really actively researched some of her hockey art:

"I did a work depicting Emile Francis and the entire Ranger bench," said the petite, green-eyed artist. "They were kind enough to let me sit directly across the ice from the bench, behind the safety glass. I was really nervous for a moment, because it looked as though they were going to sit me in the penalty box, where the photographers work. I had a vivid picture of myself sitting there avidly sketching and getting hit with a flying puck!"

At that moment Mary Jo stopped to pat "Gump" Worsley's pads and made an apt commentary on the life-like quality of her work.

"I recently returned from a trip abroad," she said, "and after I had been home awhile, I suddenly felt terrible: I realized that I had forgotten to say hello to Gump when I walked into the apartment."

SPECIAL BONUS SECTION

ARE HOCKEY'S TOUGH GUYS TURNING SOFT?

JOHNNY Ferguson had to laugh. He was in Stockholm in September 1972 with Team Canada; the assistant manager, no less. On the ice, Rangers captain Vic Hadfield, who later was to quit Team Canada, belabored a Swedish player with his stick. A week later other members of Team Canada, who were not so tough in the National Hockey League, went about the ice trying to intimidate the Russian National skaters.

Ferguson had good reason to laugh.

When Fergie roamed the NHL as "policeman" of the Montreal Canadiens he never picked his spots. He was laughing because these so-called tough guys suddenly were messing with the European types who believe fighting is *not* part of hockey.

Ferguson must have chuckled when the Rangers' Rod Gilbert, of all people, started looking for trouble. Fergie remembered that when he had played against Gilbert, Rod was one colossal zip. Nothing! Now that Ferguson is retired Gilbert has scored like he never had before. Intimidation is a big thing in hockey.

The question is, what has happened to all the intimidators? All of a sudden they seemed to have disappeared. Have hockey's tough guys turned soft? I, for one, am beginning to wonder. Take a few "for instances."

Once upon a time Boston's hockey club was known as "The Big Bad Bruins." No more. Not with a Nick Beverley wearing Teddy Green's number six. "We're the Big, *Good* Bruins now," Bobby Orr says. And maybe he's right, now that Johnny McKenzie, Gerry Cheevers, and Green are gone to the World Hockey Association. Or, take another example:

Early last season the Chicago Black Hawks played the Rangers at Madison Square Garden. An interesting situation unfolded. Cliff Koroll of the Black Hawks bumped

Rangers goalie Gil Villemure by mistake and Villemure by mistake brushed Koroll with his stick. Koroll shoved the goal keeper, then eased off.

But former Ranger defenseman Curt Bennett, seeing the collision, charged to the scene and flailed away at the unsuspecting Hawk. To say that Bennett beat Koroll to a pulp may be the understatement of the half-century. The Chicago forward was almost dead; or so it appeared as blood covered his entire face.

If John Ferguson had been a member of the Black Hawks at the time, he would have been over the boards and on Bennett's back before you could say "Clarence Campbell" and a high requiem mass would have been said for the Ranger the following day.

What makes me wonder whether the Black Hawks, as an example, turned soft was the armada of so-called tough guys on their team—Keith Magnuson, Jerry Korab, and even Stan Mikita. Where the devil were they when their buddy was getting killed? It's a question that puzzled *Chicago Tribune* writer Bob Verdi, who blasted the Black Hawks right off the sports page.

"What was appalling," wrote Verdi, "was the timidity exhibited by the Hawks when one of their own teammates was besieged by a surprise assault. Nary a Hawk on the ice budged to assist Koroll, a disappointing example of 'Fight 'em, buddy . . . we'll hold your coat.'

Many of the Rangers thought the Hawks had turned soft in this scene. Others wondered just what went through their minds. "Bennett went to the aid of Villemure, didn't he?" said Glen Sather of the Rangers. "What he did is worth more than putting the puck in the net."

Nice words, yet where was Sather when Ace Bailey and Derek Sanderson of the Bruins were beating the beehozis out of the Rangers in the Stanley Cup playoffs in 1972? Sather was conspicuous by his inconspicuousness.

For years, members of the Bruins have snidely regarded the Rangers as a chicken hockey club. It goes back to the days when Ted Green speared Phil Goyette without retaliation; and later when Green twice beat up Arnie Brown. And it continued regularly until the end of last season when Ken Hodge destroyed Vic Hadfield, who supposedly is a good fighter. Only defenseman Brad Park of the Rangers had consistently fought—and beat—the Bruins.

But Park had been sidelined that night in November 1972 when, it appeared, the Ranger tough guys turned chicken. New York was playing the Blues in St. Louis when Garry Unger speared Rangers defenseman Ab De-Marco in the back with an upwards swipe of his stick, then dropping him to his knees with a hard crosscheck that sent DeMarco to the hospital.

The St. Louis Blues, armed with tough hombres such as Bob and Barclay Plager, Andre Dupont, Jack Egers, and Steve Durbano, were not the Chicago Black Hawks. And maybe that, more than anything, explains why nobody on the Rangers went after Unger. Except with their mouths.

"It was disgraceful that the Rangers let Unger get away with that," said a newsman covering the game. "You'd never have seen Unger pull that against the Bruins."

Oh, sure, the Rangers made threatening gestures—in the safety of their dressing room. They beefed about Unger and the fact that he didn't get a penalty for his viciousness.

"It's bad enough to see that bleeping Unger pull a thing like that," said Rangers general manager-coach Emile Francis, "spearing a guy in the back and then following up with a crosscheck, but to see him get away with it makes it even tougher to swallow."

Two ironic episodes followed the Unger-DeMarco incident. The following day Unger visited DeMarco in the hospital. "I hope it's not too serious," said Unger, who presented his victim with two books. Whereupon Francis said: "Maybe someday when Unger comes to New York, DeMarco will visit *him* in a hospital." Soon, Unger and DeMarco were teammates on the Blues.

The second ironic episode occurred a couple of weeks later. Francis traded Curt Bennett, his toughest player, to the Atlanta Flames.

Who knows? Maybe toughness in hockey is going out of style. Perhaps there is no place for a Johnny Ferguson or a Teddy Green and their roughneck behavior of yesteryear. And maybe some of the so-called tough-guys are being exposed as you-know-whats. In November, Bryan Watson of Pittsburgh pasted Vic Hadfield in a Madison

Square Garden fight whereupon both were penalized. Seconds later, Glen Sather, who once was Watson's pal on the Penquins, skated past the penalty box. "Hey," snapped Watson to Sather, "I thought you told me this guy Hadfield was tough!"

In fact, I'm beginning to wonder just what constitutes toughness after all.

Some years ago I was assigned to do a story on Bobby Baun. At the time he was a rather young, violent defenseman for the Toronto Maple Leafs and one of the toughest skaters in the National Hockey League. In Toronto, of course, he was a hero. But in the five other NHL cities (this was before expansion) he was the type of opponent the fans loved to hate.

This was especially true in New York, where he would belabour various members of the rather meek and mild-mannered Rangers while the home crowd roared its displeasure. As a long-time Ranger fan I had witnessed some of Baun's, shall we say, or you would say if you were a Rangers fan, "atrocities." And so I was prepared for someone who was a cross between Genghis Khan and Attila the Hun.

Instead, I found a polite and low-keyed professional hockey player who spoke matter-of-factly about the time he had scored the winning goal in a Stanley Cup game while playing with a broken leg, but who talked with animation about the theatre in Toronto, his culinary pursuits, and his interest in the history of World War I.

Which goes to prove, I think, that some of hockey's "villains" are really not villains at all, but simply men doing a job as best they know how. And if some people get hurt in the process, including themselves, well, so be it. Hockey, after all, is a violent game, and you have to protect your own. That's the code of hockey. That, I think, was Baun's code and the code of enforcer-type players such as Orland Kurtenbach, captain of the Vancouver Canucks. But there are others with a different attitude . . .

Keith Magnuson, the Chicago Black Hawks defenseman . . .

"I like to hit," Magnuson says. "It's sort of my job, y'know—they call me the team policeman. We have some of the smallest forwards in the NHL, and I don't like to see them get pushed around. To tell the truth, I get a bigger kick out of hitting than scoring goals."

So far, Magnuson has had more than 200 stitches in his face. While playing hockey at the University of Denver he studied karate and judo. One presumes it was part of his program for entry into the NHL.

"They want me to fight," Magnuson says of the Chicago fans who egg him on from their seats in aging Chicago Stadium. "And I've never turned my back on a brawl yet."

Which is probably true. So that, plus his red hair and pugnacious attitude means that Magnuson is a marked man whenever he skates onto enemy ice. He qualifies as one of hockey's most hated players, at least among the fans. Among the players it's a different story.

"Has Magnuson ever won a fight?" asks Toronto's Eddie Shack, who is tough but really too flakey to be a true villain. "I've never seen him win one. Has Magnuson ever tied a fight?"

Then there are the players who became "bad guys" simple because there was no other way for them to remain in the NHL. Reggie Fleming, now playing for the Chicago Cougars in The World Hockey Association, is one. John McKenzie, who moved to the WHA's Vancouver Blazers is another.

McKenzie started out as a rodeo cowboy riding two thousand-pound brahma bulls and he bounced around between the NHL and assorted minor league teams from 1958 until 1963, when he finally caught on with the Black Hawks.

"A lot of guys never made the NHL because they were scared off by the minors," McKenzie says. "But maybe those guys were born scared anyway."

McKenzie was traded by the Black Hawks to the Rangers back in 1965. That was like sending a kid from reform school into a seminary. "I wasn't a finesser like them other Rangers," McKenzie says, with something approaching total disdain. "I looked out of place on ice." After a year in New York he was traded to Boston and there he found a home.

Oh, the joy of slamming into the corners, elbows moving, stick high. Hit this guy, nail that one. As the Bruins got better, McKenzie started scoring goals, more than he ever thought were possible. But he remained a hitter, the first guy into a fight. He did not forget his hockey up- bringing. That's what they paid him for, to hit people, to instill fear in his opponents.

That's why in 1970 he was voted the most popular player on the Bruins by the Boston fans. Not Bobby; not Espo; but little John McKenzie, with the type of face you'd love to punch, from the safety of a ten dollar seat, of course.

"I'm getting older now, and I admit I'm more conscious of injuries, too," McKenzie says. "But not when I'm on the ice. As soon as you start shying off, you get hurt. Then you wonder, what am I doing here, and it's time to quit. I still think I hit as hard as I always did. And when I hit a guy it's nothing personal.

"I never think of an opposing player as a guy I like or dislike," McKenzie continues. "I can fight with a guy on the ice and then go out drinking with him after the game. I've been in so many fights over the years I've learned to leave them on the ice. Your ice personality has nothing to do with the type of guy you are off the ice."

Reggie Fleming and John McKenzie are very much alike. They're both short and squat. Neither skates that well. Like McKenzie, Fleming bounced around a lot be- fore catching on for good in the NHL. But when he did arrive he was wise enough to realize at once that the only way he would last was by hitting people, by being a bad guy, an enforcer. He probably had his best times with the Rangers, whose fans looked on anyone who hit an oppos- ing player (this again was in the mid-1960s) as a revela- tion.

"I didn't like it," McKenzie says of his role as one of hockey's villains, "but you can't always be what you want. My biggest problem was trying to convince my mother I wasn't as bad as all the papers said I was. She said she didn't bring me up to be rough like that. I had to call her after every game so she wouldn't worry."

If it is difficult to imagine John Ferguson calling his mother after a game or going out for a post-game drink with a guy he had fought perhaps an hour earlier, that's mainly because it's doubtful Ferguson's opponent would be in any shape for a post-game drink.

Ferguson, in fact, was probably the most hated by enemy fans and most feared by opposing players. Pat Jordan, writing in *Sport Illustrated* once, described Ferguson this way:

"He had reaped more penalites, been in more fights and been a party to more injuries than probably any other player in the NHL. On the ice Ferguson did not seem to skate or move, he just appeared suddenly like an ill omen down from nowhere. Seconds later, there would be a fight, a penalty, an injury, and Ferguson would be gone."

Ferguson did not score many goals but he probably was as much responsible for Montreal's success as any player on the team. When the Canadiens upset the Bruins in the first round of the 1971 Stanley Cup playoffs it was the presence of Ferguson that kept the Boston Bully Boys from taking too many liberties with Les Canadiens.

Conversely, with Ferguson no longer playing, the New York Rangers dumped Montreal in the first round of 1972 Stanley Cup play. When Ferguson was active he tormented and intimidated New York's Rod Gilbert to the point where Gilbert was useless. But in the 1972 Stanley Cup games Gilbert was a key man in the Rangers' victory.

Ferguson also tormented and intimidated a great many other players. He went about his work like a professional assassin, doing what had to be done neatly, efficiently, and without a great deal of emotion. When he retired it could truly be said of him that he would not be missed—except by the Canadiens and their fans.

At one point the NHL's premier villain was Derek Sanderson. But then he got rich, and became a lot tamer. Sanderson really does not hurt people. He irritates them. He works at being hated. No doubt he enjoys hitting opponents and certainly he has never backed away from a fight. And he can enrage fans to the point where they try to do him physical harm. But you get the feeling with Sanderson that in the long run he is doing it all simply because it will mean more money.

In fact, as you look around big-league hockey today there really aren't that many players who could qualify as true bad guys. The Plager brothers are getting old. Teddy

Green has reformed. Oh, Brad Park has something going with the Boston fans because of some uncomplimentary remarks about their beloved Bruins in his controversial book, *Play the Man*.

And a lot of fans around the league hate Bobby Orr simply because he's always beating their guys.

And perhaps New York Islanders fans could work up a good hate for Phil Esposito after what he did to young Tom Miller's insides with the butt end of his stick last season. And Ranger fans tried to get good and angry with Garry Unger of St. Louis after he hospitalized Ab DeMarco in November 1972.

But Park . . . Orr . . . Esposito and Unger all are earning six-figure salaries. And it's pretty hard to hate a guy making that much money. They're superstars. And you don't hate superstars the way you'd hate a Fleming . . . or McKenzie. Even the young toughies such as Steve Durbano, Phil Russell, John Schella, Jerry Korab, and Phil Roberto seem more concerned with money.

"All I cared about was hockey," McKenzie says. "Today everything is moneyized. Young players bring their lawyers and agents with them at contract time.

"Maybe it's better for them, but I don't know whether it would have been better for me when I was younger. Pretty soon hockey players will be playing just for money instead of for the love of the game."

Did he say pretty soon?

THE STANLEY CUP SAGA

THAT huge silver mug with the oversized base being carried around the Chicago Stadium ice by captain Henri Richard of the victorious Montreal Canadiens last Spring wasn't always that huge or that awesome. In fact, The Stanley Cup had a very modest beginning.

It cost anywhere between $28.80 and $48.67, depending on which historian you believe, and was donated by Lord Stanley of Preston, Canada's Governor-General before the turn of the century. Curiously, Lord Stanley couldn't have cared less about hockey, but his son, Arthur, was a genuine ice buff and persuaded his father to buy the hunk of silver in 1893 and donate it to the "best hockey team in the world."

In those days, The Cup was strictly for amateurs, and wasn't available for professional competition until 1912, when the Quebec Bulldogs captured the prize. Up until that point The Stanley Cup endured a series of episodes that could match the Perils of Pauline.

For example, following the 1905 series won by a team known as the Ottawa Silver Seven, the victors carried The Cup home after a rather wild celebration. Harry Smith, one of the victors, had consumed enough grape to suddenly perceive The Stanley Cup as a silvery football. When Smith's entourage arrived at the Rideau Canal, Harry delivered a place-kick by the light of the silvery moon that sent The Cup arching into the canal, where it remained overnight.

The next morning, Smith began to suspect he was guilty of a rather rash place-kick. He quickly dressed, dashed to the Rideau Canal, and there he found The Cup, nestled in the bone-dry bed.

The dents that Harry's boot provided in The Cup's hide weren't to be its last. A year later, the Montreal Wanderers captured the championship and proudly, and somewhat more soberly, hauled The Cup to Jimmy Rice's Montreal photo studio. There, they proudly lined up for the traditional victory portrait, with The Stanley Cup standing before the victorious Wanderers.

When Jimmy Rice supplied the final click of the shutter, the Wanderers gleefully filed out of the studio to the nearest pub. It was time for a libation or two. Perhaps the visions of malt hops were dancing in their heads. But whatever it was, the Wanderers jubilantly departed and never gave a thought to the trophy.

In fact, for months nobody but a charwoman did. When the last of the Wanderers had left the studio, the cleaning lady noticed the interesting silver cup sitting on the floor.

"My," she must have said, "but this would make a lovely flower pot." So, she took The Stanley Cup home.

Several months later, the Wanderers management thought it would be a noble gesture if The Stanley Cup were placed on display in the victors' arena. But, alas, where was the trophy? The last place anyone remembered seeing it was at Jimmy Rice's studio. Jimmy was contacted. He called his charwoman, who explained that The Stanley Cup was on the mantel over the fireplace—literally in full bloom!

In 1924, the Montreal Canadiens captured The Cup, and were feted by the University of Montreal in a public reception at the National Monument in Montreal. That was simple enough. Then, the Canadiens were invited to a party by Canadiens' owner Leo Dandurand at the boss's home. But before they got there, The Cup managed to escape. Here's how it happened, in Dandurand's words:

"Georges Vezina, Sprague Cleghorn, Sylvio Mantha and I got into a Model T Ford to make the trip. The little lizzy stalled going up Cote St. Antoine Road in Westmount and we all got out to push.

"Cleghorn, who had been jealously carrying The Cup in his lap, deposited it on the curb at the roadside before he joined us in shoving the car up the hill. When we reached the top, we hopped back into the car and resumed our hockey chatter as we got going again.

"Upon reaching my house, we all started in on a big bowl of punch which my wife had prepared. It wasn't until she asked, 'Well ... where is this Stanley Cup you've been talking about?' that we realized Cleghorn had left it on the side of the road.

"Sprague and I drove hurriedly back to the spot almost an hour after we had pushed the car up the hill. There was The Cup, in all its shining majesty, still sitting on the curb of the busy street!"

As The Cup grew older, it grew proportionately in size. In order to inscribe it, it became necessary to enlarge the base of the trophy again and again until it more than quadrupled its original size. And as the trophy grew, greater and greater security measures were taken to protect it from thieves and short-memoried players. But, still,

The Cup managed to get away only to be found again. Occasionally, it was the center of rather bizarre rites.

In 1940, The Cup was the subject of just such an improbable scene. As Ranger manager Lester Patrick looked on, the Madison Square Garden mortgage was set aflame and completely burned right inside the bowl of The Stanley Cup.

During the playoffs of April 1962 The Cup resided in a huge glass case right in the midst of the Chicago Stadium lobby for all to see. The Black Hawks had won the world championship the previous year and were now engaged in another furious battle for the trophy.

A Montreal fan by the name of Ken Kilander took a dim view of The Stanley Cup residing in Chicago. He studied the silver mug and the glass case with the intensity of a safecracker about to launch the great heist. And then he did it. Kilander opened the glass case and, to his supreme amazement, neither gongs nor sirens nor any form of warning buzzer sounded.

Well, this was just wonderful. He gingerly reached in and plucked The Cup off its stand. Still there was not a sound. Now there was just one thing to do—leave! And that he did. Nursing The Cup with affection, Kilander sauntered through the lobby of Chicago Stadium and headed for the exit doors. It was almost too good to be true.

Kilander was just a few yards from freedom when a stadium cop spotted him and wondered just what he might have in mind, carrying The Stanley Cup out of the Chicago arena.

Kilander's retort will never win him entrance into *Bartlett's Familiar Quotations*, abridged or unabridged, but it did get prizes for sincerity. "I want to take it back where it belongs," he explained, "to Montreal."

Being a Chicagoan, the cop disagreed. He returned The Cup where it belonged, at least for another week, to the glass case.

In recent years The Cup has continued to have its ups and downs. It disappeared again during the 1970-71 season, and before Toronto police could find it, a campaign was launched by Boston's "Sports Huddle" radio show, urging the Royal Canadian Mounted Police onto the case. As always, The Cup reappeared in time.

Since the Canadiens won the prize last season, The Cup has led a relatively quiet life. But, based on past performance, by next fall it could wind up anywhere from Toronto to Timbuktu.

FBI MAN OF THE NHL
By Roberto Borea

STAN Mikita was returning to his hotel room following the 1970 All-Star game up in Boston when he noticed out of the corner of his eye that Frank Torpey, the newly appointed National Hockey League security boss, was stepping out of the elevator. Jokingly, Mikita turned and said: "Hey Frank, last Friday you told us you weren't going to be following us around. Here it is Monday, I look over my shoulder and there you are."

Torpey replied, "Well Stan, you're a special case. I was told to keep an eye on you."

Chicago's crack center laughed and continued walking down the corridor to his room. As he put the key in the door he suddenly realized that Torpey's room was across the way. Speaking a little more nervously this time, Mikita asked, "You're kidding aren't you? I'm not a special case am I?"

As it developed, Mikita was not a special case and the location of the rooms was purely coincidental. When NHL president Clarence Campbell and a committee of the League Board of Governors established the new security department and hired Frank Torpey, a retired FBI agent, to head it in November 1970, the last thing on their minds was a surveillance network to keep tabs on the activities of hockey players.

The National Hockey League has not been tainted by any major gambling scandal since 1948 and league officials were determined that the good record should be maintained. The baseball world was rocked in 1919 by the Blacksox scandal and it suffered the burden of a Denny McLain; pro football has had its Paul Hornung and Alex Karras.

It is Torpey's job to make sure that the NHL is spared any similar occurence. With fifteen commendations for meritorious service from the late J. Edgar Hoover under his belt, Torpey is clearly up to the job.

"I'm not a miracle-maker capable of stopping anything that comes along," he asserted cautiously, "but I'm going to do my damndest to protect the integrity of the game."

In addition to protecting against gambling scandal, the NHL security department directs its attention towards investigating a hockey player's potential business partners if the player requests it, and toward improving the physical security of the league arenas.

Torpey's assistant is Irv Blehm, a former member of the Royal Canadian Mounted Police. Although he originally worked out of the Manhattan office, Blehm has since been transferred to Toronto. In addition, the department has security representatives, usually retired law enforcement officers from the local police or the FBI, who are employed on a "moderate retainer" basis and paid on a per diem rate for their investigative work.

"Their job is to keep their ears to the ground in their particular city," Torpey explained, "to ensure that any problem concerning the NHL is brought to our attention.

"The basic orientation of the *'depaatment'* is prevention," he added with an accent that announced his Bostonian upbringing. "We work on the principle that in professional sports it doesn't do you a damn bit of good to wait until the problem occurs and then make an investigation. We like to prevent the problem from occuring in the first place."

Torpey continually emphasized that his function was not that of a "league cop," and he admits some of the players were a bit sceptical when the program was first announced.

He explained, "The first thing I did when I came on

board was to go around to each team and introduce myself and spell out what we had in mind. I'm sure a few
players were suspicious at first. Maybe they felt, 'Aw,
we're getting a con job here.' "

But Torpey quickly adds that "Over the two and a half
years the department has been in existence we've managed
to convince everyone that we're not the league cop, and
we don't intend to follow any players around and check
on their girlfriends.

"Our primary concern is to help the players, to protect
their careers, and to save the league from possible embarrassment. As far as I know we have not had any embarrassing problems," Torpey said proudly.

Rumor had been circulating that certain members of
the Chicago Black Hawks were not always playing with
the team's interest at heart during the 1961-62 season.
The allegation emerged during an inquiry being conducted
by the Police Commission of Quebec in an effort to deter-
mine the influence of organized crime in the province. One
witness who took the stand claimed to have received information that the Chicago Black Hawks goalie had placed
bets against his team. No names were mentioned, the
reference clearly was to the club's only goal tender at the
time.

When asked about this incident Torpey did not flatly re-
ject it, but he did indicate doubts as to the credibility of
the witness. He said, "The individual is a self-professed
former bookmaker and he was convicted of fraud in Quebec, for which he was sentenced to ten years in jail. The
guy ended his testimony by saying he feels everything in
sports is fixed; now, anybody in their right mind knows
that's not true."

Torpey also alluded to editorial criticism of the inquiry
which sees it as little more than a forum for character as-
sassination. Pointing out that the witness failed to back his
claims, Torpey added, "I don't approve of someone getting up on the stand and making charges without any substantiation. Lacking substantiation by the individual, I'll
leave it up to the league whether they want an investigation of something that may have occurred eleven years
ago."

The last publicized incident along the same lines occurred in 1948 when the New York Rangers' Billy Taylor and the Boston Bruins' Don Gallinger were permanently exiled from hockey by Campbell "for conduct detrimental to hockey and for associating with a known gambler."

Wiretap evidence gathered by the Detroit Police Department allegedly revealed that the two had placed bets against their own teams.

In 1970 the NHL Board of Governors, spurred by a crusading campaign led by Toronto writer Scott Young, raised the ban. Gallinger and Taylor, ages forty-four and fifty-one, respectively, were not in a position to take advantage of the League's beneficence.

Babe Pratt, motivated by financial difficulties, turned to gambling in 1946 and was suspended for his enterprise. When it was revealed sixteen days later that Pratt had never bet against his Toronto teammates he was reinstated.

Every September Torpey travels to all the team training camps in the league for a meeting with the players, trainers, and coaches. He reviews such league rules as the one which prohibits gambling on hockey games and cautions everyone on each team to be very careful about whom they associate with.

"My job is to educate the players to the fact that they could be contacted by a big-time gambler," Torpey explained. "I tell them what to look for in these types of contacts. Big-time gamblers are pretty smooth operators. I try to tell the players how a big-time gambler could approach them; in other words, give them certain signs that they can recognize as an approach and hopefully through this type of education forestall any problems or any close relationship from developing."

Professional gamblers, realizing that $100,000 does not guarantee a fix, and cognizant of existing stringent sports legislation, prefer to go with the odds, and inside information gives a big edge. An unpublicized injury to a star, dissension among the players, or any other factor that could affect a team's performance is what a gambler tries to glean from a casual conversation at the bar with an unsuspecting athlete.

While Torpey cannot prevent "security leaks" of this sort, he does make a concerted effort during his visits to impress upon the players a basic rule of thumb. "We advise the players that if a fellow wants to talk about hockey, they should only talk about games already completed and not about future games or anything going on within the clubs.

"We also caution the players to be careful about the places they frequent because of the knowledge we have of some of the people who hang out in certain locations."

But Torpey hastens to add that the league does not have an official list of verboten spots for hockey players. Rather, lists are drawn up by the local security representatives, "who are very knowledgeable about their own towns," and then presented to the general managers with the recommendation that they tell their players to stay away.

While neither Torpey nor his security representatives follow players around, information is occasionally received that a player has been seen in the company of an undesirable. In such instances, Torpey said, "we go to him and explain why we feel the association is not in his best interest. This has not happened often but when it does the player receives the advice well. In all instances the player had no idea of what the individual's background was, and when informed he severed the acquaintanceship."

When asked about the drug problem, Torpey replied quickly, "This is an area of great concern for everyone in organized sports. We're very fortunate in that in hockey we have not had any drug problems. I have been told, by what I consider to be highly reliable sources, that hockey players are not involved in the drug scene at all."

This has not led to any false sense of security however. In fact, a new program scheduled to take effect this season, has been developed in an effort to establish some kind of uniformity to the dispensation of drugs by NHL teams. Trainers and team doctors will be required to maintain a record of drugs dispensed to the players, and when Torpey visits each club an audit of the drug inventory will be made and checked off against the records.

Torpey's department also delves into an area that most other sports security organizations do not touch. Last season his office conducted a survey of each arena in the league "from the standpoint of reducing the possibility of fans and players getting involved in a confrontation."

"We don't want the players going into the stands, and we don't want the fans harassing the players while they are on or leaving the ice. We want to avoid what happened last year with the Minnesota North Stars," Torpey declared.

The results of the survey were forwarded to Campbell and subsequently made available to each club. Where possible, suggested changes have been carried out. At Madison Square Garden, for example, an enclosure was built last year during the Ranger-Chicago Stanley Cup semi-final playoffs over the ramp area where the visiting clubs and league officials enter and leave the ice. In Pittsburgh, Torpey's recommendation that the goal judge be protected by a glass cage has been followed.

In addition to the annual training camp visit, Torpey makes it a point to visit each team at least once during the season. "If I go to a game I drop in to see the players and coach and say hello. This is to let them know I am in the area," he explained.

"But I don't want to scare them or give the impression that I'm following them. It's a good idea to let them know I am around, because if they see me perhaps some of the things we've said during training camp will come back. It enhances our program."

While regretting that he does not know each of the 300-plus NHL players personally, Torpey does pride himself on the fact that he recognizes most of them either by name or by sight. "I find them to be just terrific kids," said Torpey, with a paternal smile.

Torpey is also quite friendly with hockey's lepers—the officiating staff. John D'Amico, the only Italian linesman in the league, has left proof positive of his last visit to security headquarters. Placed conspicuously on the wall is a sheet of paper with a hand outlined on it. The warning declares, "The Family was here" and underneath the hand a parenthetical note adds, "An offer you can't refuse."

When asked whether his interest in hockey predated his job with the NHL, Torpey replied, "I was born and raised in Boston and you can't be born and raised there and not have an interest in hockey."

Upon graduation from Boston College in 1952, Torpey joined the army, serving with the artillery corps in Korea. After returning to the States he began an eleven-year stint with the FBI.

Of the fifteen meritorious service citations he received, the ones that meant the most were awards for continued investigatory achievement over a period of time. While admitting that he misses "the thrill of the chase, Torpey says that he finds his new career to be "extremely interesting."

Torpey's hobbies center around his children, two boys and two girls, and the whole family shares his love for hockey. In fact, the Torpey family faces internal strife; the older boy, Michael, is a Ranger fan, while Mark is a Bruin partisan.

The NHL security chief also admits to "dabbling in local politics." As he explained it, "Besides hockey, politics is something a kid grows up with in Boston. I became involved in the local Republican Party in Rockland County where I live, not so much from the standpoint of what I could get out of it, but rather to try and keep some of the politicians on the level." Presently he is the district chairman of the Republican Party in Clarkestown.

Shortly after retiring from the Bureau, Torpey took a stab at running for Sheriff of Rockland County. The effort was unsuccessful because, as Torpey put it, "I was strictly a law enforcement officer and not a politician."

Torpey has no regrets however, for he notes, with a broad smile and a twinkle in his light blue eyes, that, "This was probably the best break I ever had." Judging by the clean slate he has maintained during his tenure as security chief it was a good break for the National Hockey League as well.

THE STATISTICS

APPS, SYLVANUS MARSHALL (SYL) JR.

Born, Toronto, Ont., August 1, 1947.
Center. Shoots right. 6', 185 lbs.
Last amateur club: Kingston Frontenacs (Srs.).

Season	Club	Lea	GP	G	A	TP	PIM	GP	G	A	TP	PIM
1968-69	Buffalo	AHL	2	1	2	3	4	--	--	--	--	--
1969-70	Omaha	CHL	68	16	38	54	43	12	*10	9	*19	4
1969-70	Buffalo	AHL	--	--	--	--	--	7	2	3	5	6
1970-71	NY Rangers	NHL	31	1	2	3	11	--	--	--	--	--
1970-71	Omaha	CHL	11	0	5	5	4	--	--	--	--	--
1970-71	Pittsburgh	NHL	31	9	16	25	21	--	--	--	--	--
1971-72	Pittsburgh	NHL	72	15	44	59	78	4	1	0	1	2
1972-73	Pittsburgh	NHL	77	29	56	85	18	--	--	--	--	--
	NHL Totals		211	54	118	172	128	4	1	0	1	2

Traded to Pittsburgh by N.Y. Rangers for Glen Sather, January 26, 1971.

CHEEVERS, GERALD MICHAEL (GERRY)

Born, St. Catharines, Ont., December 7, 1940.
Goaltender. Shoots left. 5'11", 185 lbs.
Last amateur club: St. Michael's College (Jrs.).

Season	Club	Lea	GPI	GA	SO	GAPG	GPI	GA	SO	GAPG
1961-62	Toronto	NHL	2	7	0	3.50	--	--	--	--
1961-62a	Sault Ste. Marle	CPHL	29	103	1	3.55	--	--	--	--
1961-62	Pitt.-Rochester	AHL	24	84	1	3.50	2	8	0	4.00
1962-63	Rochester	AHL	19	75	1	3.95	--	--	--	--
1962-63a	Sudbury	EPHL	51	212	4	4.15	8	29	*1	3.62
1963-64a	Rochester	AHL	66	187	3	2.84	2	8	0	4.00
1964-65ab	Rochester	AHL	72	195	*5	2.68	10	24	0	2.34
1965-66	Boston	NHL	7	34	0	6.00	--	--	--	--
1965-66.	Oklahoma City	CPHL	30	73	3	2.49	9	19	0	*2.11
1966-67	Boston	NHL	22	72	1	3.33	--	--	--	--
1966-67c	Oklahoma City	CPHL	26	71	1	2.80	11	29	*1	*2.64
1967-68d	Boston	NHL	47	125	3	2.83	4	15	0	3.75
1968-69	Boston	NHL	52	145	3	2.80	9	16	*3	1.68
1969-70e	Boston	NHL	41	108	4	2.72	13	29	0	2.23
1970-71	Boston	NHL	40	109	3	2.72	6	21	0	3.50
1971-72d	Boston	NHL	41	101	2	2.50	8	21	*2	2.61
	NHL Totals		252	701	16	2.86	40	102	5	2.51
1972-73	Cleveland	WHA	52	149	5	2.83	9	22	0	2.44
	WHA Totals		52	149	5	2.83	9	22	0	2.44

a Received one assist.
b Won Harry "Hap" Holmes Memorial Trophy
c Won CPHL Leading Goalkeeper Award.
d Received two assists.
e Received one assist in playoffs.
Drafted by Boston from Toronto, June 9, 1965.

CLARKE, ROBERT EARLE (BOBBY)

Born, Flin Flon, Man., August 13, 1949.
Center. Shoots left. 5'10", 180 lbs.
Last amateur club: Flin Flon Bombers (Jrs.).

Season	Club	Lea	GP	G	A	TP	PIM	GP	G	A	TP	PIM
				Regular Schedule					Playoffs			
1969-70	Philadelphia	NHL	76	15	31	46	68	—	—	—	—	—
1970-71	Philadelphia	NHL	77	27	36	63	78	4	0	0	0	0
1971-72	Philadelphia	NHL	78	35	46	81	87	—	—	—	—	—
1972-73	Philadelphia	NHL	78	37	67	104	80	11	2	6	8	6
		NHL Totals	309	114	180	294	313	15	2	6	8	6

a Won Hart Trophy.

COURNOYER, YVAN SERGE

Born, Drummondville, Que., November 22, 1943.
Right wing. Shoots left. 5'7", 165 lbs.
Last amateur club: Canadiens (Jrs.).

Season	Club	Lea	GP	G	A	TP	PIM	GP	G	A	TP	PIM
				Regular Schedule					Playoffs			
1963-64	Mtl. Canadiens	NHL	5	4	0	4	0	—	—	—	—	—
1964-65	Quebec	AHL	7	2	1	3	0	—	—	—	—	—
1964-65	Mtl. Canadiens	NHL	55	7	10	17	10	12	3	1	4	0
1965-66	Mtl. Canadiens	NHL	65	18	11	29	8	10	2	3	5	2
1966-67	Mtl. Canadiens	NHL	69	25	15	40	14	10	2	3	5	6
1967-68	Mtl. Canadiens	NHL	64	28	32	60	23	13	6	8	14	4
1968-69	Mtl. Canadiens	NHL	76	43	44	87	31	14	4	7	11	5
1969-70	Mtl. Canadiens	NHL	72	27	36	63	23	—	—	—	—	—
1970-71	Mtl. Canadiens	NHL	65	37	36	73	21	20	10	12	22	6
1971-72	Mtl. Canadiens	NHL	73	47	36	83	15	6	2	1	3	2
1972-73	Mtl. Canadiens	NHL	67	40	39	79	18	17	15	10	25	2
		NHL Totals	611	276	259	535	163	102	44	45	89	27

DRYDEN, KENNETH WAYNE (KEN)

Born, Hamilton, Ont., August 8, 1947.
Goaltender. Shoots left. 6'4", 210 lbs.
Last amateur club: Canadian National Team.

Season	Club	Lea	GPI	GA	SO	GAPG	GPI	GA	SO	GAPG
				Regular Schedule				Playoffs		
1970-71	Mtl. Voyageurs	AHL	33	84	3	2.68	—	—	—	—
1970-71	Mtl. Canadiens	NHL	6	9	0	1.65	20	61	0	3.00
1971-72	Mtl. Canadiens	NHL	64	142	8	2.24	6	18	0	—
1972-73	Mtl. Canadiens	NHL	54	119	6	2.26	17	52	1	3.06
		NHL Totals	124	270	14	2.22	43	131	1	3.05

a Received one assist in playoffs.
b Won Conn Smythe Trophy.

ESPOSITO, PHILIP ANTHONY (PHIL)

Born, Sault Ste. Marie, Ont., February 20, 1942.
Center. Shoots left. 6'1", 210 lbs.
Last amateur club: St. Catharines (Jrs.).

Season	Club	Lea	Regular Schedule					Playoffs				
			GP	G	A	TP	PIM	GP	G	A	TP	PIM
1961-62	Sault Ste. Marie	EPHL	6	0	3	3	2	—	—	—	—	—
1962-63	St. Louis	EPHL	71	36	54	90	51	—	—	—	—	—
1963-64	St. Louis	CPHL	43	26	54	80	65	—	—	—	—	—
1963-64	Chicago	NHL	27	3	2	5	2	4	0	0	0	0
1964-65	Chicago	NHL	70	23	32	55	44	13	3	3	6	15
1965-66	Chicago	NHL	69	27	26	53	49	6	1	1	2	2
1966-67	Chicago	NHL	69	21	40	61	40	6	0	0	0	7
1967-68	Boston	NHL	74	35	*49	84	21	4	0	3	3	0
1968-69b	Boston	NHL	74	49	*77	*126	79	10	*8	*10	*18	8
1969-70d	Boston	NHL	76	*43	56	99	50	14	*13	*14	*27	16
1970-71ace	Boston	NHL	78	*76	76	*152	71	7	3	7	10	6
1971-72a	Boston	NHL	76	66	67	133	76	15	9	15	24	24
1972-73	Boston	NHL	78	55	75	130	87	2	0	1	1	2
	NHL Totals		691	398	500	898	519	81	37	54	91	80

a Won Art Ross Trophy.
b Won Hart Trophy.
c NHL record for points in regular season.
d NHL record for points in Stanley Cup Playoffs (shared with Frank Mahovlich).
e NHL record for goals in regular season.
Traded to Boston by Chicago with Ken Hodge and Fred Stanfield for Gilles
Marotte, Pit Martin and Jack Norris, May 15, 1967.

HODGE, KENNETH RAYMOND (KEN)

Born, Birmingham, England, June 25, 1944.
Right wing. Shoots right. 6'2", 216 lbs.
Last amateur club: St. Catharines Black Hawks (Jrs.).

Season	Club	Lea	Regular Schedule					Playoffs				
			GP	G	A	TP	PIM	GP	G	A	TP	PIM
1964-65	Buffalo	AHL	2	0	2	2	0	4	0	0	0	4
1964-65	Chicago	NHL	1	0	0	0	2	—	—	—	—	—
1965-66	Chicago	NHL	63	6	17	23	47	5	0	0	0	8
1966-67	Chicago	NHL	69	10	25	35	59	6	0	0	0	4
1967-68	Boston	NHL	74	25	31	56	31	4	3	0	3	4
1968-69	Boston	NHL	75	45	45	90	75	10	5	7	12	4
1969-70	Boston	NHL	72	25	29	54	87	14	3	10	13	7
1970-71	Boston	NHL	78	43	62	105	113	7	2	5	7	6
1971-72	Boston	NHL	60	16	40	56	81	15	9	8	17	*62
1972-73	Boston	NHL	73	37	44	81	58	5	1	0	1	7
	NHL Totals		565	207	293	500	553	66	23	30	53	100

Traded to Boston by Chicago with Phil Esposito and Fred Stanfield for Gilles
Marotte, Pit Martin and Jack Norris, May 15, 1967.

HULL, ROBERT MARVIN (BOBBY)

Born, Point Anne, Ont., January 3, 1939.
Left wing. Shoots left. 5'10", 193 lbs.
Last amateur club: St. Catharines Black Hawks (Jrs.).

Season	Club	Lea	GP	G	A	TP	PIM	GP	G	A	TP	PIM
					Regular Schedule					Playoffs		
1957-58	Chicago	NHL	70	13	34	47	62	—	—	—	—	—
1958-59	Chicago	NHL	70	18	32	50	50	6	1	1	2	2
1959-60a	Chicago	NHL	70	*39	42	*81	68	3	1	0	1	2
1960-61	Chicago	NHL	67	31	25	56	43	12	4	10	14	4
1961-62a	Chicago	NHL	70	*50	34	*84	35	12	*8	5	13	12
1962-63	Chicago	NHL	65	31	31	62	27	5	*8	2	10	4
1963-64	Chicago	NHL	70	*43	44	87	50	7	2	5	7	2
1964-65bc	Chicago	NHL	61	39	32	71	32	14	*10	7	*17	27
1965-66ac	Chicago	NHL	65	*54	43	*97	70	6	2	2	4	10
1966-67	Chicago	NHL	66	*52	28	80	52	6	4	2	6	0
1967-68	Chicago	NHL	71	*44	31	75	39	11	4	6	10	15
1968-69	Chicago	NHL	74	*58	49	107	48	—	—	—	—	—
1969-70	Chicago	NHL	61	38	29	67	8	8	3	8	11	2
1970-71	Chicago	NHL	78	44	52	96	32	18	11	14	25	16
1971-72	Chicago	NHL	78	50	43	93	24	8	4	4	8	6
	NHL Totals		1036	604	549	1153	640	116	62	66	128	102
1972-73	Winnipeg	WHA	63	51	52	103	37	14	9	16	25	—
	WHA Totals		63	51	52	103	37	14	9	16	25	—

a Won Art Ross Trophy.
b Won Lady Byng Memorial Trophy.
c Won Hart Trophy.

MacLEISH, RICHARD GEORGE (RICK)

Born, Lindsay, Ont., January 3, 1950.
Center. Shoots left. 5'11", 175 lbs.
Last amateur club: Peterborough Petes (Jrs.).

Season	Club	Lea	GP	G	A	TP	PIM	GP	G	A	TP	PIM
					Regular Schedule					Playoffs		
1970-71	Oklahoma City	CHL	46	13	15	28	93	—	—	—	—	—
1970-71	Philadelphia	NHL	26	2	4	6	19	4	1	0	1	0
1971-72	Philadelphia	NHL	17	1	2	3	9	—	—	—	—	—
1971-72	Richmond	AHL	42	24	11	35	33	—	—	—	—	—
1972-73	Philadelphia	NHL	78	50	50	100	69	10	3	4	7	2
	NHL Totals		121	53	56	109	97	14	4	4	8	2

Traded to Philadelphia by Boston with Danny Schock for Mike Walton, February 1, 1971.

MAHOVLICH, FRANCIS WILLIAM (FRANK)

Born, Timmins, Ont., January 10, 1938.
Left wing. Shoots left. 6′, 205 lbs.
Last amateur club: St. Michael's College (Jrs.).

Season	Club	Lea	GP	G	A	TP	PIM	GP	G	A	TP	PIM
1956-57	Toronto	NHL	3	1	0	1	2	—	—	—	—	—
1957-58a	Toronto	NHL	67	20	16	36	67	—	—	—	—	—
1958-59	Toronto	NHL	63	22	27	49	94	12	6	5	11	18
1959-60	Toronto	NHL	70	18	21	39	61	10	3	1	4	27
1960-61	Toronto	NHL	70	48	36	84	131	5	1	1	2	6
1961-62	Toronto	NHL	70	33	38	71	87	12	6	6	12	*29
1962-63	Toronto	NHL	67	36	37	73	56	9	0	2	2	8
1963-64	Toronto	NHL	70	26	29	55	66	14	4	*11	15	20
1964-65	Toronto	NHL	59	23	28	51	76	6	0	3	3	9
1965-66	Toronto	NHL	68	32	24	56	68	4	1	0	1	10
1966-67	Toronto	NHL	63	18	28	46	44	12	3	7	10	8
1967-68	Toronto	NHL	50	19	17	36	30	—	—	—	—	—
	Detroit	NHL	13	7	9	16	2	—	—	—	—	—
1968-69	Detroit	NHL	76	49	29	78	38	—	—	—	—	—
1969-70	Detroit	NHL	74	38	32	70	59	4	0	0	0	2
1970-71bc	Detroit	NHL	35	14	18	32	30	—	—	—	—	—
	Mtl. Canadiens	NHL	38	17	24	41	11	20	*14	13	*27	18
1971-72	Mtl. Canadiens	NHL	76	43	53	96	36	6	3	2	5	2
1972-73	Mtl. Canadiens	NHL	78	38	55	93	51	17	9	14	23	6
	NHL Totals		1110	502	521	1023	1009	131	50	65	115	163

a Won Calder Memorial Trophy.
b NHL record for goals in Stanley Cup Playoffs.
c NHL record for points in Stanley Cup Playoffs (shared with Phil Esposito).
Traded to Detroit by Toronto with Gary Unger, Pete Stemkowski and rights to
Carl Brewer for Paul Henderson, Norm Ullman and Floyd Smith, March 3,
1968. Traded to Montreal by Detroit for Mickey Redmond, Guy Charron and Bill
Collins, January 13, 1971.

MARTIN, HUBERT JACQUES (PIT)

Born, Noranda, Que., December 9, 1943.
Center. Shoots right. 5′8″, 165 lbs.
Last amateur club: Hamilton Red Wings (Jrs.)

Season	Club	Lea	GP	G	A	TP	PIM	GP	G	A	TP	PIM
1961-62	Detroit	NHL	1	0	1	1	0	—	—	—	—	—
1962-63	Pittsburgh	AHL	5	1	2	3	0	—	—	—	—	—
1963-64	Pittsburgh	AHL	21	3	7	10	2	—	—	—	—	—
1963-64	Detroit	NHL	50	9	12	21	28	14	1	4	5	14
1964-65	Detroit	NHL	58	8	9	17	32	3	0	1	1	2
1965-66	Pittsburgh	AHL	16	6	6	12	26	—	—	—	—	—
1965-66	Detroit	NHL	10	1	1	2	0	—	—	—	—	—
	Boston	NHL	41	16	11	27	10	—	—	—	—	—
1966-67	Boston	NHL	70	20	22	42	40	—	—	—	—	—
1967-68	Chicago	NHL	63	16	19	35	36	11	3	6	9	2
1968-69	Chicago	NHL	76	23	38	61	73	—	—	—	—	—
1969-70a	Chicago	NHL	73	30	33	63	61	8	3	3	6	4
1970-71	Chicago	NHL	62	22	33	55	40	17	2	7	9	12

1971-72	Chicago	NHL	78	24	51	75	56	8	4	2	6	4
1972-73	Chicago	NHL	78	29	61	90	30	16	10	6	16	6
	NHL Totals		660	198	291	489	406	77	23	29	52	44

a Won Bill Masterton Memorial Trophy.
Traded by Detroit to Boston for Parker MacDonald, December 30, 1965. Traded to Chicago by Boston with Gilles Marotte and Jack Norris for Phil Esposito, Ken Hodge and Fred Stanfield, May 15, 1967.

MIKITA, STANLEY

Born, Sokolce, Czechoslovakia, May 20, 1940.
Center. Shoots right. 5'9", 165 lbs.
Last amateur club: St. Catharines (Jrs.).

			Regular Schedule					Playoffs			
Season	Club	Lea	GP	G	A	TP	PIM	GP	G	A	TP	PIM
1958-59	Chicago	NHL	3	0	1	1	4	--	--	--	--	--
1959-60	Chicago	NHL	67	8	18	26	119	3	0	1	1	2
1960-61	Chicago	NHL	66	19	34	53	100	12	*6	5	11	21
1961-62	Chicago	NHL	70	25	52	77	97	12	6	*14	*21	19
1962-63	Chicago	NHL	65	31	45	76	69	6	3	2	5	2
1963-64a	Chicago	NHL	70	39	50	*89	146	1	3	6	9	8
1964-65a	Chicago	NHL	70	28	*59	*87	154	14	3	7	10	*53
1965-66	Chicago	NHL	68	30	*48	78	58	6	1	2	3	2
1966-67abc	Chicago	NHL	70	35	*62	*97	12	6	2	2	4	2
1967-68abc	Chicago	NHL	72	40	47	*87	14	11	5	7	12	6
1968-69	Chicago	NHL	74	30	67	97	52	--	--	--	--	--
1969-70	Chicago	NHL	76	39	47	86	50	8	4	6	10	2
1970-71	Chicago	NHL	74	24	48	72	85	18	5	13	18	16
1971-72	Chicago	NHL	74	26	39	65	46	8	3	1	4	4
1972-73	Chicago	NHL	57	27	56	83	32	15	7	13	20	2
	NHL Totals		976	401	673	1074	1038	126	48	80	128	139

a Art Ross Trophy.
b Hart Trophy.
c Lady Byng Trophy.

ORR, ROBERT GORDON (BOBBY)

Born, Parry Sound, Ont., March 20, 1948.
Defense. Shoots left. 5'11", 185 lbs.
Last amateur club: Oshawa Generals (Jrs.).

			Regular Schedule					Playoffs			
Season	Club	Lea	GP	G	A	TP	PIM	GP	G	A	TP	PIM
1966-67a	Boston	NHL	61	13	28	41	102	--	--	--	--	--
1967-68b	Boston	NHL	46	11	20	31	63	4	0	2	2	2
1968-69b	Boston	NHL	67	21	43	64	133	10	1	7	8	10
1969-70bcefg	Boston	NHL	76	33	*87	*120	125	14	9	11	20	14
1970-71bcdfh	Boston	NHL	78	37	*102	139	91	7	5	7	12	25
1971-72bfg	Boston	NHL	76	37	80	117	106	15	5	*19	24	19
1972-73b	Boston	NHL	63	29	72	101	99	5	1	1	2	7
	NHL Totals		467	181	432	613	719	55	21	47	68	77

a Won Calder Memorial Trophy.
b Won James Norris Memorial Trophy.
c NHL record for goals in regular season by a defenseman.
d NHL record for assists in regular season.
e Won Art Ross Trophy.
f Won Hart Trophy.
g Won Conn Smythe Trophy.
h Won Lou Marsh Trophy as Top Canadian Athlete.

PARK, DOUGLAS BRADFORD (BRAD)

Born, Toronto, Ont., July 6, 1948
Defense. Shoots left. 6', 190 lbs.
Last amateur club: Toronto Marlboros (Jrs.)

Season	Club	Lea	Regular Schedule					Playoffs				
			GP	G	A	TP	PIM	GP	G	A	TP	PIM
1968-69	Buffalo	AHL	17	2	12	14	49	--	--	--	--	--
1968-69	NY Rangers	NHL	54	3	23	26	70	4	0	2	2	7
1969-70	NY Rangers	NHL	60	11	26	37	98	5	1	2	3	11
1970-71	NY Rangers	NHL	60	7	37	44	114	13	0	4	4	42
1971-72	NY Rangers	NHL	75	24	49	73	130	16	4	7	11	21
1972-73	NY Rangers	NHL	52	10	43	53	51	10	2	5	7	8
	NHL Totals		309	55	178	233	463	48	7	20	27	89

PERREAULT, GILBERT

Born, Victoriaville, Que., November 13, 1950.
Center. Shoots left. 6', 195 lbs.
Last amateur club: Montreal Canadiens (Jrs.)

Season	Club	Lea	Regular Schedule					Playoffs				
			GP	G	A	TP	PIM	GP	G	A	TP	PIM
1970-71a	Buffalo	NHL	78	38	34	72	19	--	--	--	--	--
1971-72	Buffalo	NHL	76	26	48	74	24	--	--	--	--	--
1972-73	Buffalo	NHL	78	28	60	88	10	6	3	7	10	2
	NHL Totals		232	92	142	234	53	6	3	7	10	2

a Won Calder Memorial Trophy.

RATELLE, JOSEPH GILBERT YVON JEAN

Born, Lac St. Jean, Que., October 3, 1940.
Center. Shoots left. 6'1", 175 lbs.
Last amateur club: Guelph Royals (Jrs.)

Season	Club	Lea	Regular Schedule					Playoffs				
			GP	G	A	TP	PIM	GP	G	A	TP	PIM
1959-60	Three Rivers	EPHL	3	3	5	8	0	4	0	3	3	0
1960-61	NY Rangers	NHL	3	2	1	3	0	--	--	--	--	--
1961-62	NY Rangers	NHL	31	4	8	12	4	--	--	--	--	--
1961-62	Kitch.-Waterloo	EPHL	32	10	29	39	8	7	2	6	8	2
1962-63	NY Rangers	NHL	48	11	9	20	8	--	--	--	--	--
1962-63	Baltimore	AHL	20	11	8	19	0	3	0	0	0	0
1963-64	Baltimore	AHL	57	20	26	46	2	--	--	--	--	--
1963-64	NY Rangers	NHL	15	0	7	7	6	--	--	--	--	--
1964-65	Baltimore	AHL	8	9	4	13	6	--	--	--	--	--
1964-65	NY Rangers	NHL	54	14	21	35	14	--	--	--	--	--
1965-66	NY Rangers	NHL	67	21	30	51	10	--	--	--	--	--
1966-67	NY Rangers	NHL	41	6	5	11	4	4	0	0	0	2
1967-68	NY Rangers	NHL	74	32	46	78	18	6	0	4	4	2
1968-69	NY Rangers	NHL	75	32	46	78	26	4	1	0	1	0
1969-70	NY Rangers	NHL	75	32	42	74	28	6	1	3	4	0
1970-71a	NY Rangers	NHL	78	26	46	72	14	13	2	9	11	8
1971-72b	NY Rangers	NHL	63	46	63	109	4	6	0	1	1	0
1972-73	NY Rangers	NHL	78	41	53	94	12	10	2	7	9	0
	NHL Totals		702	267	377	644	148	49	6	24	30	12

a Won Bill Masterton Memorial Trophy.
b Won Lady Byng Memorial Trophy.

REDMOND, MICHAEL EDWARD (MICKEY)

Born, Kirkland Lake, Ont., December 27, 1947.
Right wing. Shoots right. 5'11", 185 lbs.
Last amateur club: Peterborough Petes (Jrs.)

Season	Club	Lea	GP	G	A	TP	PIM	GP	G	A	TP	PIM
1967-68	Houston	CPHL	15	9	8	17	9	—	—	—	—	—
1967-68	Mtl. Canadiens	NHL	41	6	5	11	4	2	0	0	0	0
1968-69	Mtl. Canadiens	NHL	65	9	15	24	12	14	2	3	5	2
1969-70	Mtl. Canadiens	NHL	75	27	27	54	61	—	—	—	—	—
1970-71	Mtl. Canadiens	NHL	40	14	15	29	35	—	—	—	—	—
	Detroit	NHL	21	6	8	14	7	—	—	—	—	—
1971-72	Detroit	NHL	78	42	29	71	34	—	—	—	—	—
1972-73	Detroit	NHL	76	52	41	93	24	—	—	—	—	—
	NHL Totals		396	156	140	296	177	16	2	3	5	2

Traded to Detroit by Montreal with Guy Charron and Bill Collins for Frank
Mahovlich, January 13, 1971.

SAVARD, SERGE A.

Born, Montreal, Que., January 22, 1946.
Defense. Shoots left. 6'2", 200 lbs.
Last amateur club: Montreal Canadiens (Jrs.)

Season	Club	Lea	GP	G	A	TP	PIM	GP	G	A	TP	PIM
1964-65	Omaha	CPHL	2	0	0	0	0	4	0	1	1	4
1966-67	Mtl. Canadiens	NHL	2	0	0	0	0	—	—	—	—	—
1966-67	Quebec	AHL						1	0	0	0	2
1966-67a	Houston	CPHL	68	7	25	32	155	5	1	3	4	17
1967-68	Mtl. Canadiens	NHL	67	2	13	15	34	6	2	0	2	0
1968-69b	Mtl. Canadiens	NHL	74	8	23	31	73	14	4	6	10	24
1969-70	Mtl. Canadiens	NHL	64	12	19	31	38	—	—	—	—	—
1970-71	Mtl. Canadiens	NHL	37	5	10	15	30	—	—	—	—	—
1971-72	Mtl. Canadiens	NHL	23	1	8	9	16	6	0	0	0	10
1972-73	Mtl. Canadiens	NHL	74	7	32	39	58	17	3	8	11	25
	NHL Totals		341	35	105	140	249	43	9	14	23	59

a Won CPHL Rookie-of-the-Year Award.
b Won Conn Smythe Trophy.

STAPLETON, PATRICK JAMES (PAT)

Born, Sarnia, Ont., July 4, 1940.
Defense. Shoots left. 5'8", 185 lbs.
Last amateur club: St. Catharines Teepees (Jrs.)

Season	Club	Lea	GP	G	A	TP	PIM	GP	G	A	TP	PIM
1959-60	Buffalo	AHL	1	0	0	0	2	—	—	—	—	—
1960-61	Sault Ste. Marie	EPHL	59	5	43	48	22	12	1	8	9	2
1961-62	Boston	NHL	69	2	5	7	42	—	—	—	—	—
1962-63	Kingston	EPHL	49	10	26	36	92	5	4	2	6	12
1962-63	Boston	NHL	21	0	3	3	8	—	—	—	—	—
1963-64	Portland	WHL	70	5	44	49	80	5	1	6	7	0
1964-65a	Portland	WHL	70	29	57	86	61	10	3	4	7	16
1965-66	St. Louis	CPHL	14	2	4	6	6	—	—	—	—	—

1965-66	Chicago	NHL	55	4	30	34	52	6	2	3	5	4
1966-67	Chicago	NHL	70	3	31	34	54	6	1	1	2	12
1967-68	Chicago	NHL	67	4	34	38	34	11	0	4	4	4
1968-69	Chicago	NHL	75	6	50	56	44	—	—	—	—	—
1969-70	Chicago	NHL	49	4	38	42	28	—	—	—	—	—
1970-71	Chicago	NHL	76	7	44	51	30	18	3	14	17	4
1971-72	Chicago	NHL	78	3	38	41	47	8	2	2	4	4
1972-73	Chicago	NHL	75	10	21	31	14	16	2	15	17	10
	NHL Totals		635	43	294	337	353	65	10	39	49	38

a Won WHL Leading Defenseman Award.

Drafted by **Boston** from **Chicago**, June 1961. Traded by **Boston** with Orland Kurtenbach and Andy Hebenton to **Toronto** for Ron Stewart, June 8, 1965. Drafted by **Chicago** from **Toronto**, June 9, 1965.

VICKERS, STEPHEN JAMES (STEVE)

Born, Toronto, Ont., April 21, 1951.
Right wing. Shoots left. 5'11", 180 lbs.
Last amateur club: Toronto Marlboros (Jrs.)

			Regular Schedule					Playoffs				
Season	Club	Lea	GP	G	A	TP	PIM	GP	G	A	TP	PIM
1971-72	Omaha	CHL	70	36	23	59	45	—	—	—	—	—
1972-73a	NY Rangers	NHL	61	30	23	53	37	10	5	4	9	4
	NHL Totals		61	30	23	53	37	10	5	4	9	4

a Won Calder Trophy.

WARD, RONALD LEON (RON)

Born, Cornwall, Ont., September 12, 1944.
Center. Shoots right. 5'10", 180 lbs.
Last amateur club: Cornwall Royals (Jrs.)

			Regular Schedule					Playoffs				
Season	Club	Lea	GP	G	A	TP	PIM	GP	G	A	TP	PIM
1965-66	Tulsa	CPHL	69	6	22	28	37	7	1	2	3	9
1966-67	Tulsa	CPHL	42	12	15	27	46	—	—	—	—	—
1967-68	Phoenix	WHL	1	0	1	1	0	—	—	—	—	—
1967-68	Tulsa	CPHL	67	31	*54	*85	30	11	5	5	10	8
1968-69a	Rochester	AHL	73	35	43	78	18	—	—	—	—	—
1969-70	Toronto	NHL	18	0	1	1	2	—	—	—	—	—
1969-70	Phoenix	WHL	22	7	9	16	12	—	—	—	—	—
1969-70	Tulsa	CPHL	22	7	17	24	15	—	—	—	—	—
1970-71	Rochester	AHL	69	23	16	39	33	—	—	—	—	—
1971-72	Vancouver	NHL	71	2	4	6	4	—	—	—	—	—
	NHL Totals		89	2	5	7	8	—	—	—	—	—
1972-73	NY Raiders	WHA	77	51	67	118	28	—	—	—	—	—
	WHA Totals		77	51	67	118	28	—	—	—	—	—

a Won Dudley (Red) Garrett Memorial Trophy.

Drafted by **Vancouver** from **Toronto** in Expansion Draft, June 10, 1970.